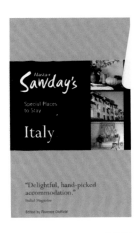

Alastair
Sawday's

Special Places
to Stay

Italy

"Delightful, hand-picked
accommodation."
Italian Magazine

Edited by Florence Oldfield

Special Places
to Stay

Spain

"Indispensable."
Evening Standard

Alastair
Sawday's

Special Places
to Stay

French Châteaux
& Hotels

"Sawday unearths the
most beguiling châteaux,
auberges and hotels."
The Daily Telegraph

ipa
Publisher
of the Year

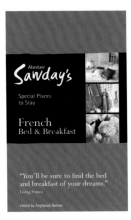

Alastair
Sawday's

Special Places
to Stay

French
Bed & Breakfast

"You'll be sure to find the bed
and breakfast of your dreams."
Living France

Edited by Ampharad Barnes

Alastair
Sawday's

Special Places to Stay

Fifth edition
Copyright © 2011
Alastair Sawday Publishing Co. Ltd
Published in 2011
ISBN-13: 978-1-906136-42-0

Alastair Sawday Publishing Co. Ltd,
The Old Farmyard, Yanley Lane,
Long Ashton, Bristol BS41 9LR, UK
Tel: +44 (0)1275 395430
Email: info@sawdays.co.uk
Web: www.sawdays.co.uk

The Globe Pequot Press,
P. O. Box 480, Guilford,
Connecticut 06437, USA
Tel: +1 203 458 4500
Email: info@globepequot.com
Web: www.globepequot.com

Series Editor Alastair Sawday
Editor Kathie Burton
Assistants to Editor Polly Procter,
Alex Skinner
Editorial Director Annie Shillito
Publishing Manager Jackie King
Photo processing Alec Studerus
Writing Jo Boissevain, Kathie Burton,
Monica Guy
Inspections Kathleen Becker, Carol
Dymond, Lauren Wojtyla
Sales & Marketing
Rob Richardson, 01275 395433
PR Sarah Bolton, 01275 395433

Maps: Maidenhead Cartographic Services
Printing: Butler Tanner & Dennis, Frome
UK distribution: Penguin UK, London
Production: The Content Works

Cover photo credits
1. iStockphoto.com/ra-photos 2. iStockphoto.com/ShyMan 3. iStockphoto.com/Manuela Ferreira

Alastair
Sawday's

Special Places
to Stay

Portugal

4 Contents

Photo: Quinta da Vila Francelina, entry 22

This tiny country of just ten million people, the poorest in Western Europe, once ruled much of the world. Its explorers, searching for a route to India, came across Africa, India, the islands of South East Asia, and went on to China and Brazil. Wherever they went they established colonies, and kept them too long. They only let go of Macau in 1999. It took a peaceful revolution in 1975 for them to overthrow their dictator Salazar, and finally to abandon their African colonies.

A world-travelled Portugal can show us an architecture that is exhilarating. There are Moorish and Oriental influences, African and Brazilian – and hints of more. A walk around Lisbon reveals traditions and ideas from all over the world. Those weary of cultural sameness delight in the refreshing, if ancient, differences between Portugal and the rest of Europe. And there is a gentle reticence, too, about the Portuguese. They are proud of being very different from their Spanish neighbours.

I am always exhilarated by this Portuguese-ness, the tension between the grandly astonishing history and the apparent domesticity of modern Portugal. In a day you can admire the magnificence of, say, the Abbey of Batalha and eat simple fisherman's food on the coast in a modest resort. Modesty is part of being Portuguese. Perhaps my favourite evening there was spent listening to *fado* in a restaurant. It was sad, wistful, low-key but beautiful and passionate. Perhaps those words capture my view of the country.

So a holiday in Portugal is full of delightful surprises and this book takes you to beautiful places and fascinating people who have held out against the tide.

'Our' owners are fiercely independent, utterly themselves. Be bold in Portugal; travel about with this book and meet these people. It is a richly varied strip of Iberia. And be prepared for it to get under your skin.

Alastair Sawday

Photo left: Monte Saraz, entry 56
Photo right: Monte Velho Nature Resort, entry 66

There's much to celebrate in our Special Places — landscapes, histories, houses — but perhaps the strongest feature of our books is the people in them. There's an old-world gentility about the Portuguese that you will discover when you stay, for life is lived at a slower pace. Indeed, "the Portuguese hour" is not dissimilar to the Irish — along with the famous charm.

Over the years we have made our way from the north to the south of this small, richly endowed country, from the 'Wuthering Heights' of Alta Minho to the sand-kissed Algarve. There is much to love: the ancient agricultural landscapes, the atmospheric, occasionally crumbling, architecture, the lush valleys, the wild coasts and the 220 days of sunshine a year. Portugal is a country to travel through slowly, so give yourself time.

Take the Alentejo, Portugal's biggest region, which covers almost a third of the country. Just two hours from Lisbon you can be blissfully remote, in amongst the cork and holm oaks, the storks and the sunflowers. Indeed, you can walk for miles without seeing a soul, until you chance upon some remote 'tasca' for a tipple of 'medronho' and a slice of 'porco preto'. Visitors with gastronomic leanings often linger longer than intended within Portugal's borders.

The Beira province to the north is equally untouched; the Serra da Estela is Portugal's highest range. Vineyards, orchards, pine forests and waterfalls abound, as do Dao wine and mountain cheeses. This region is hiker and biker heaven, and you can ski in Torre.

Portugal's economy may be in the doldrums, but tourism is holding its own, thanks largely to the Algarve, one of the world's top twenty travel destinations. The long-standing cork industry, on the other hand, fares less well, as competition from plastic takes its toll. In its place is the ubiquitous eucalyptus, a cash crop (paper and pulp) with undesirable side effects: combustibility in high summer and a root system that removes nutrients and water from the soil.

On a positive note Portugal, thanks to its geographical bounty, is fast becoming a leader in renewable energy. The world's largest photovoltaic plant is at Amareleja (seven hours of sunshine per day) while the country's potential for wind and hydro energy is exciting; wind farms are popping up on every windswept spot, including World Heritage spot Sintra.

You'll find an unusually eclectic gathering of places in this new edition — an agroturismo in subtropical Madeira, a charming townhouse in the heart of Tavira, a rustic-chic farmhouse between Silves and the sea. Have fun with this book: it is an open-sesame to houses and people so read carefully above and between the lines to find which places would best suit you. Happy travelling — and, as ever, let us know how you get on.

Photo: Rio Arade Manor House, entry 75

It's simple. There are no rules, no boxes to tick. We choose places that we like and are subjective in our choices. We look for comfort, originality, authenticity; the way guests are treated comes as high on our list as the setting, the atmosphere and the food.

Inspections

Our inspectors, too, know their patch – they all live in Portugal and are integrated into Portuguese life, unearthing little gems to add to our stable and alerting us to those against whom we should bolt the door. They don't take a clipboard and don't have a list of what is acceptable and what is not.

Instead, they chat for an hour or so with the owner, look round – closely – and, if the visit happens to be the last of the day, they stay the night. It's all very informal, but it gives us an excellent idea of who would enjoy staying there – after all, our aim is to match places with guests. Once in the book, properties are re-inspected every three to four years so that we can keep things fresh and accurate.

Feedback

The accuracy of our books depends on what you, not only our inspectors, tell us. Your feedback is invaluable and we always act upon comments, so write, email or use the forms on our website.

Photo: Hotel Martinhal, entry 67

However, please do not tell us if the bedside light was broken or the bedding felt damp (note, dehumidifiers do brisk business in Portugal). Tell the owner, immediately, and get them to do something about it! Most owners will bend over backwards to help.

What to expect

This guide to mainland Portugal and Madeira contains a fascinating mix of B&Bs, guest houses, agroturismos and hotels as well as self-catering villas, cottages and apartments.

Maps

If you know which region you want to stay in, our maps are your best guide; if you only consult the regional headings in the book you may miss a gem in a neighbouring region just over the border. Numbered properties are flagged on the map and coloured to show whether they are B&Bs/hotels or self-catering properties. Dual-coloured flags denote that they do both. They're a great starting point for planning your trip, but please don't use them as anything other than a general guide.

Types of property

There are many clues as to what to expect in the property name alone so it's worth explaining them all.

- Albergaria: an upmarket inn
- Cabana: a hut
- Casa: a house, old or new
- Castelo: a castle

Photo: Kazuri Garden Cottages, entry 81

- Estalagem: an inn, more expensive than an albergaria
- Herdade: a large farm or estate
- Monte: a long, low Alentejo farmhouse, usually on top of a hill
- Paço: a palace or country house
- Palacio: a palace or country house that is grander than a paço
- Pensão: a guest house, the Portuguese equivalent of a bed and breakfast, although breakfast is not always included in the price
- Quinta: a country estate or villa; in the Douro wine-growing area it often refers to a vineyard
- Fortaleza: a fort
- Residencial: a town guest house, slightly more expensive than a pensão, usually serving breakfast
- Solar: a manor house

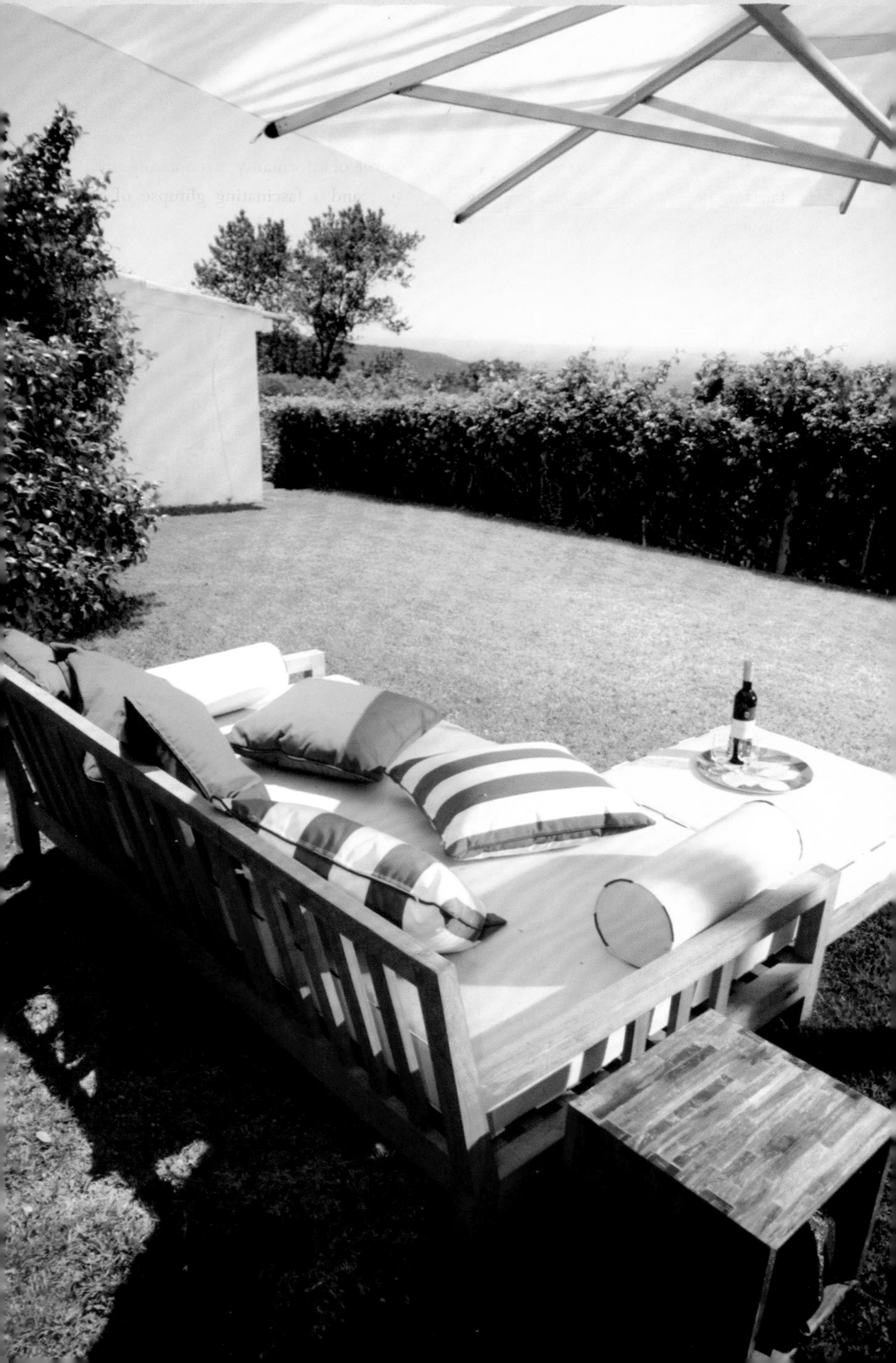

Tourist Definitions are listed below; you'll often see these marked on blue road signs.

- Turismo de habitacão: B&B in a stately home
- Turismo rural: B&B in a simpler home
- Agroturismo: B&B on a farm
- Casa de campo: simple rural private house
- Hotel rural: a country hotel

B&Bs

B&Bs, however grand, are people's homes, not hotels. You'll most probably have breakfast and dinner with your hosts and/or fellow guests, and the welcome will be personal. Some owners give you a front door key so you may come and go as you please; others like to have the house empty between, say, 10am and 4pm.

Do expect
- a personal welcome
- a willingness to go the extra mile
- a degree of informality, even family-life chaos, and a fascinating glimpse of a Portuguese way of life

Don't be dismayed if you don't find
- a lock on your bedroom door
- your room cleaned and your bed made every day
- a private table at breakfast and dinner
- an immediate response to your booking enquiry

An 'agroturismo' is a B&B on a working farm, and the outbuildings are often converted to take self-catering guests too; this is increasingly popular. Farmer-owners often offer good value short breaks so check when booking. A

Photo above: Quinta de São Vicente, entry 5
Photo left: Quinta das Nascentes Altas, entry 65

Bathrooms – The vast majority of bedrooms in this book are en suite (ie. you don't have to go outside your room to get to it). Only if a bedroom has a shared or private but separate bathroom do we list bathroom details.

Sitting rooms – Most hotels have one or two communal areas, while most B&Bs offer guests the family sitting room to share, or provide a sitting room specially for guests. If neither option is available we generally say so, but do check. Do not assume that every bedroom or sitting room has a TV.

'residencial' is an urban B&B, usually set right in the heart of a town and with hotel-like facilities.

Hotels

Those we choose normally have fewer than 50 rooms; many are family-run with friendly staff and in old buildings, others have a boutique feel. An 'albergaria' is a small, upmarket inn – usually offering excellent value for money.

Rooms

We tell you if a room is a single, double, twin/double (ie. with zip and link beds), suite (a room with space for seating), family (a double bed + single beds), or triple (three single beds) – and whether they are in the main building or in apartments, suites or cottages. Ask your host for more details and you'll find they often have a flexible approach, particularly to families and their needs.

Photo above: Quinta da Vila Francelina, entry 22
Photo right: Estalagem da Ponta do Sol, entry 101

Meals

Unless we say otherwise, breakfast is included, simple or extravagant. Some owners are fairly unbending about breakfast times, others are happy just to wait until you want it, or even bring it to you in bed.

Apart from breakfast, no meals should be expected unless you have arranged them in advance. Many B&Bs offer their guests dinner, usually an opportunity to get to know your hosts and to make new friends among the other guests. We indicate the distance to the nearest restaurant when dinner isn't offered.

Meal prices are per person and when wine is included this can mean a range of things, from a standard quarter-litre carafe per person to a barrel of table wine; from a decent bottle of local wine to an excellent estate wine.

Prices

Each entry gives a price PER ROOM per night for two people; self-catering prices are mostly quoted per week. The price range covers a night in the cheapest room in low season to the most expensive in high season. Some owners charge more at certain times (during festivals, for example) and some charge less for stays of more than one or two nights. Some owners ask for a two-night minimum stay and we mention this where possible; many offer special deals for three-night stays.

Prices quoted are those given to us for 2011–2013 but are not guaranteed, so double-check when booking.

Symbols

There is an explanation of these on the inside back cover of the book. Use them as a guide, not as a statement of fact. However, things do change: bikes may be under repair or a new pool may have been put in. If an owner does not have the symbol that you're looking for, it's worth discussing your needs.

Note that the 🐦 symbol shows places which are happy to accept children of all ages; it does not mean that they will necessarily have cots and high chairs. Many who say no to children do so not because they don't like them but because they may have a steep stair, an unfenced pond or they find balancing the needs of mixed age groups too challenging.

Quick reference indices

On pages 154-155 is a quick reference section to direct you to places that have, for example, double rooms for £70 or under, have wheelchair access, have a pool or places where owners will collect you from local transport.

Bookings

It is best to confirm your booking in writing. Often you will need to pay a deposit, the equivalent of one night's stay or 30% of a week's holiday. You can do this by credit card, personal cheque or bank transfer. If you make your booking by telephone, many hotels will ask you for a credit card number as an insurance against cancellation. Make sure that you have written confirmation of all you have discussed, ask for detailed directions and be clear about your dining arrangements/requirements in smaller places. Book well ahead if you plan to be in Portugal during school holidays. August is a good month to avoid the busy beaches and to head for the remoter places in this book.

Portugal is on the same time zone as the UK but if you pop across the border to Spain, it is one hour ahead.

Photo above: Yurt Holiday Portugal, entry 34
Photo right: Companhia das Culturas, entry 94

Arrivals

Many city hotels will only hold a reservation until the early evening, even if you booked months in advance. So warn them if you are planning to arrive late. It remains law that you should register on arrival but hotels have no right to keep your passport.

Tipping

Tipping is not as widespread in Portugal as in the UK and US. However, the more expensive restaurants do expect a 10% service charge, if it is not already included.

Public holidays & festivals

In Portugal many shops, businesses and restaurants in all but the busiest areas are closed at Easter, Christmas and New Year, and on the following public holidays:
February/March: Carnival Tuesday (day before Ash Wednesday)
March/April: Good Friday
25 April: Liberty Day, commemorating the 1974 Revolution
1 May: Labour Day
May/June: Corpus Christi (ninth Tuesday after Easter)
10 June: Portugal Day; Camões & the Communities Day
15 August: Feast of the Assumption
5 October: Republic Day, commemorating the 1910 declaration of the Portuguese Republic
1 November: All Saints Day
1 December: Independence Day, commemorating the 1640 restoration of independence from Spain
8 December: Feast of the Immaculate Conception

Telephones

Calling Portugal from another country: From the UK: 00 351 then the number. From the USA: 011 351 then the number.

Landline numbers begin with 2, mobile phone numbers with 9.

As well as public phone boxes (for which you can buy phone cards in most news-agents) and phone boxes inside post offices (look for Correios), virtually every café has a phone for which customers pay the 'impulsos' used, counted on a meter. Many owners answer the phone with 'estou' (which, literally translated, means 'I'm ready').

Electricity

Virtually all sockets have 220/240 AC voltage (usually 2-pin). Pack an adaptor if you are travelling with a laptop or – a boon in summer – a bedside fan.

Driving

The maps in this guide give an approximate idea of where places are; use with an up-to-date detailed road map for navigation. Avoid driving around cities and towns at rush hours on and around public holidays and, preferably, August when there is a mass exodus to the countryside and the coast. It is compulsory to have a spare set of bulbs, a warning triangle, a fire extinguisher and a basic first aid kit in the car.

It is an offence to drive without having your driving licence on you. Remember that foreign number plates attract attention in the big cities so never leave your car with valuables inside. Use a public car park; they are cheap and safe.

Auto-estradas are toll motorways (portagems), usually with two to three lanes. They are indicated by blue signs

and road numbers preceded by 'A' and are generally shown on maps with a bold double red line. Make sure you take the toll ticket.

Itinerário-principal (IP) & Itiniário complementar (IC) are the main non-toll roads; sometimes the road names change mid-route. Estradas Nacionais (national two-lane roads) are usually prefixed by an N.

Petrol is more expensive in Portugal than in the UK (and much more expensive than in the USA). Don't wait until you hit red on the gauge before filling up as you can often go for many miles, even on the biggest roads, without coming across a station.

Public transport

You can get almost everywhere by train or bus. Trains are inexpensive and some lines very scenic, but it's usually quicker to go by bus, especially for shorter journeys. Buses marked 'carreiras' (or CR) are the slow local buses. 'Expressos' are direct buses between large towns and 'rápidas' are fast regional buses. One of the quick reference indices at the back of the book, 'No car?', tells you the entry numbers for those properties you can easily reach by public transport. Make sure you discuss finer details with your host.

Food

It can be inexpensive to eat out in Portugal. The set meal, 'ementa turistica',

may offer a small choice, while à la carte, 'á lista', is a full choice. The dish of the day, 'prato do dia', is usually a local speciality and helpings can be enormous. It is perfectly fine to ask for a 'meia dose', half portion, or for two adults to ask for 'uma dose', a single portion to share.

At virtually any restaurant in Portugal you will be given bits to nibble before your meal arrives – most often olives, chouriço, sardine spread and bread – but you will be charged for whatever you eat. If you don't want it, just say so. Bacalhão, salted cod, is the national dish: there are said to be 365 different ways of preparing it! Pork, as in Spain, is also popular; the homemade vegetable soups are often good and so is fresh fish near the coast.

Photo above: Vilacampina Guesthouse, entry 88
Photo left: Cortinhas, entry 57

Many Special Places have restaurants or make authentic local dishes. The 𝒷 symbol shows those places which can provide vegetarian dinners – a welcome plus in a mainly carnivorous country.

Environment

Portugal is becoming more 'green' and most places have a recycling centre. Do try to recycle your waste. For information about the environment in Portugal check out www.naturlink.pt

Subscriptions

Owners pay to appear in this guide. Their fee goes towards the costs of inspecting, publishing, marketing and

maintaining a sophisticated website. We only include places that we like and find special for one reason or another. It is not possible for anyone to buy their way onto these pages. Nor is it possible for the owner to write their own description. We will say if the bedrooms are small, or if a main road is near. We do our best to avoid misleading readers!

Internet

Our website, www.sawdays.co.uk, has online pages for all the special places featured here and from all our other books – around 5,000 in total. There's a searchable database, a taster of the write-ups and between two and ten photos per entry. And look out for our dedicated website on self-catering in England, Scotland and Wales, www.special-escapes.co.uk. For more details, see the back of the book.

Disclaimer

We make no claims to pure objectivity in choosing these places. They are here simply because we like them. Our opinions and tastes are ours alone and this book is a statement of them; we hope you will share them. We have done our utmost to get our facts right but apologise unreservedly for any mistakes that may have crept in.

You should know that we don't check such things as fire regulations, swimming pool security or any other laws with which owners of properties receiving paying guests should comply. This is the responsibility of the owners.

Photo: Casa do Terreiro do Poço, entry 52

SPAIN

Viana do
Castelo

MINHO
• Braga

Chaves
Bragança

TRÁS-OS-MONTES
E ALTO DOURO

Vila Real

Oporto
(Porto)

DOURO
LITORAL

BEIRA ALTA

• Aveiro
• Viseu

ATLANTIC
OCEAN

• Guarda

Coimbra•
Covilhã

BEIRA LITORAL

BEIRA BAIXA

• Marinha Grande
Castelo Branco

Caldas da Rainha

• Portalegre

Santarém

ESTREMADURA

RIBATEJO

ALTO ALENTEJO

LISBON

SPAIN

• Setúbal
• Évora

• Beja

BAIXO ALENTEJO

ALGARVE

• Faro

MADEIRA   Funchal

SPAIN

Catered

Self-catered

0   10   20 kilometres
0   10 miles

Monção   Melgaço
        Longos Vales
Valença   Merufe
do Minho
Vila Nova
de Cerveira   Paredes
                   de Coura
Vila Praia   Caminha   Arcos de   Soajo   Lindoso
de Âncora   Valdevez
                                                                    Montalegre
Vila Nova   2   Ponte de Lima   4   Ponte da Barca
de Cerveira   MINHO
              3
Viana do   Boticas
Castelo   Caldelas

                                          Vieira do Minho
Esposende   Barcelos   Braga   5   Póvoa de
                                        Lanhoso   Ribeira   Bornes
                              6   Cabeceiras de Basto   de Pena   de Aguiar
Póvoa de Varzim   Vila Nova   Guimarães   8   Arco de Baúlhe   Vila Pouca
Vila do Conde   de Famalicão   7   Fafe   de Aguiar
                                                    Celorico   Mondim de Basto
                          Santo Tirso   Lagáres   de Basto   Parque
                                                                 Natural
                                              Amarante   do Alvão   Vila Real
                    Maia   11   Sabrosa
              Águas Santas   Penafiel   12   13   14   16
Oporto   9   Valongo   Mesão
(Porto)   10   Gondomar   Baião   Frio
Vila Nova de Gaia   Oliveira do   15
              Douro   Lamego   Armamar
Espinho   Cinfães
              DOURO LITORAL   Castelo de Paiva
                                                              Tarouca
Santa Maria de Feira   Burgo   Moimenta
              Vila de   Arouca   da Beira
              Cucujães   Castro Daire   21
Ovar   20
Avanca   Vila Noba
              Estarreja   de Paiva
                                      Reserva   São Pedro do Sul   BEIRA   ALTA
Gafanha da Nazare   Sever do Vouga   Botânica   Satão
              22   Albergaria-a-Velha   Vouzela
Ilhavo   Aveiro   de Cambarinho   Viseu
              23   Águeda   Fornos de Algodres
                                                              Mangualde
Miro   24   Nelas
              Anadia   Oliveira do Conde   26   Gouveia
Mealhada   Luso   Santa   Seia   28
Cantanhede   Mortágua   25   Comba Dão   Manteigas
        Pampilhosa   29
              A14/IP5   30   Parque Natural
                                        da Serra da Estrela

3   4

©Maidenhead Cartographic, 2011

Map 2

25

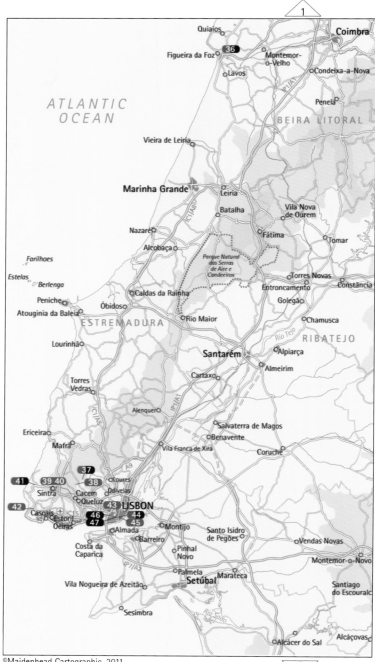

Map 4

27

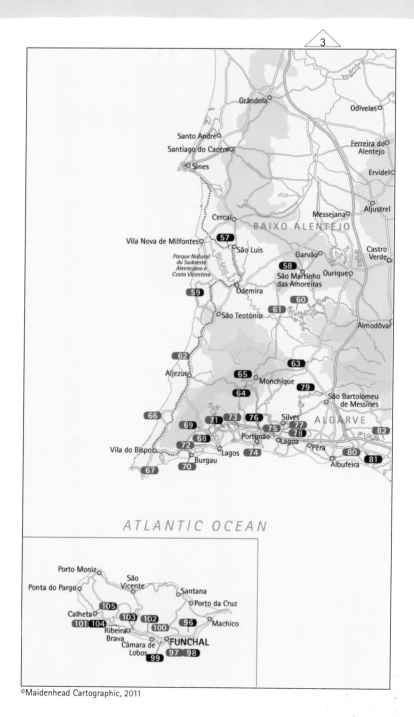

Map 6

29

Minho

Casa de Esteiró

A magical old house that reflects the outgoing personalities of owners José and Maria; an eclectic experience from the moment you arrive. Behind the electric gates, peacefully back from the road, lies this late 18th-century house, most handsome and decorated with antiques and fine furniture: traditional Portuguese mixes happily with finds from the owners' years abroad in the diplomatic service. The gallery is long, with masses of comfortable seating, beautiful cushions, porcelain, paintings, a granite fireplace. The library is exquisite, with a small chapel off it; ask about the altar carried by Great Grandfather during the Peninsular War. Bedrooms too have good fabrics and Portuguese furnishings, the finest room being the suite in the main house. Breakfast can be served in your room or in the dining room, lined with beautiful ceramics and silverware. Outside, find a good pool and a garden with specimen trees, thriving in this Minho climate... and some delightful peaceful areas for sitting and listening to the running water and birds. A river beach is a short walk and the camellias are exquisite in spring.

Price	€90-€100. Singles €50-€70. Apartments €120 per night.
Rooms	2 + 3: 1 suite (2 doubles), 1 single. 3 apartments for 2-4 in annexe.
Meals	Restaurant 200m.
Closed	Rarely.
Directions	From Viana do Castelo, A28 to Valença. Exit 3 for Moledo/Afife onto N13 to Carminha. At sign for centre, km90, turn right.

José Manuel & Maria Villas-Boas
Vilarelho,
4910-605 Caminha

Tel	+351 258 721333
Email	contacto@casaesteiro.com
Web	www.casaesteiro.com

Casa Santa Filomena

Casa Santa Filomena, a solid 1920s house tucked into a quiet corner of an already quiet village; peace is assured. When we visited in spring the old wisteria was in bloom, as pretty a welcome as you could wish for. A high wall runs around the property, girdling a small vineyard where local varieties of grape are grown. Elsewhere the profusion of flowers – roses, dahlias, azaleas, hydrangeas – is heady proof of the microclimate that this part of the Minho enjoys; breakfast juice comes from their own oranges. The Ukrainian housekeeper is charming but speaks very little English; if the owners are around, ask to see their collection of restored carriages. A swimming pool and tennis courts are a kilometre away, and wonderful beaches not much further: Afife is a favourite with bodyboarders, Praia da Arda is for surfers, and Ancora is dotted with restaurants. If you're not a watersporter, then there's walking along the dunes and around the hillside. Bedrooms are functional, comfortable and clean, with new curtains and watercolours. This is a good value place to stay. *Two nights preferred.*

Price	€50-€55. Suite €60.
Rooms	5: 4 twins/doubles, 1 suite.
Meals	Restaurants nearby. BYO wine.
Closed	Rarely.
Directions	From Valença to Viana, 1st left to Afife. From Viana 1st right. At square in centre of Afife turn inland/right (Estrada de Cabanas). House up hill on left at 1st fork.

Mary Kendall
Estrada de Cabanas 621,
Afife, 4900-012 Viana do Castelo

Tel	+351 258 981619
Email	soc.com.smiths@mail.telepac.pt

Quinta da Bouça d'Arques

In the grounds of the grand 300-year-old manor are these modern apartments; João & Ana Luisa (the family has been here for centuries) have created a stunning blend of contemporary architecture and tradition. Old stone walls, contemporary glass panels and modern art personify a minimalist chic. Splashes of colour contrast with dark antiques, striped silks hang above fine old beds, and neutral colours blend with beams, granite, terracotta and painted shutters. Baskets, blankets, ceramics and tall glass vases filled with petals add character; bathrooms have deep baths and hand-painted tiles. A woollen cushion on a carved bench, burning incense, a silk-clad mannequin – all contribute to the serenity of this place. Start the day with breakfast on your terrace, then move to wooden loungers by the pool. There are courtyards and vineyards to explore, wines to buy, surprises at every turn. Great for families, too: find a big wooden playhouse and BBQs and bikes to borrow. A 20-minute walk leads to good restaurants; Viana do Castelo is also blessed with riverine and surfing beaches. *Minimum two nights. A Rusticae property.*

Price	€75–€150 (€665–€945 per week).
Rooms	7 cottages: 6 for 2, 1 for 4.
Meals	Breakfast included. Restaurant 1km.
Closed	Never.
Directions	A28 Porto-Viana, exit 21 for Braga. At r'bout N13 for Viana do Castelo. After 4km right for Vila Verde. At blue sign for house, left, follow cobbled road; on left.

João & Ana Luisa Magalhães Couto
Rua Abreu Teixeira 333, Vila de Punhe,
4905-641 Viana do Castelo

Tel	+351 967 571524
Mobile	+351 968 044992
Email	joaomcouto@net.sapo.pt
Web	www.boucadarques.com

Casa de Pomarchão

Casa de Pomarchão goes all the way back to the 15th century but owes its present look to a rebuild of 1775 when a baroque chapel and veranda were added. The noble old manor house stands at the centre of a 60-hectare estate of vineyards and thick pine forest. Your choice is between the apartment in the main building (every inch the aristocrat's domicile) and one of seven equally charming outbuildings beyond; they range from the old stables to the olive press. Some are classical in style (Milho and Bica), others have a more rustic feel (Toca and Mato). Expect soft beds, small sofas, twin-hob kitchenettes, original fireplaces and hand-painted chairs – an appealing décor. Homemade cakes and jams are brought over for breakfast; apartments have French windows opening onto garden or terrace. Stroll the estate, take a splash in the atmospheric *tanque*, trot off down the hill for Ponte de Lima (a 30-minute walk), roast chestnuts in autumn or plan a day at the beach. Delightful Carmen greets you with a glass of vinho verde and a bowl of olives. This is a fine place run by charming people – we'd happily stay a week.

Price	Apartment €65–€70. House €115–€130 per night.
Rooms	1 apartment for 2, 7 houses for 2-4.
Meals	Restaurants a short walk.
Closed	10-30 December.
Directions	Signed 2km outside Ponte de Lima on N201 to Valença. Note: do not use satnav, do not follow signs to Arcozelo!

Frederico & Carmen Villar
Arcozelo,
4990-068 Ponte de Lima

Tel	+351 258 741742
Mobile	+351 969 134481
Email	flavv@clix.pt
Web	www.casadepomarchao.com

Entry 4   Map 1

Quinta de São Vicente

Dogs dozing in the shade set the tone; this is a flower-filled oasis, full of farm sounds and birdsong. Gentle Luis and chatty Teresa are a lovely pair and welcome you to their traditional Minho farmhouse. It's an enchanting place: relaxed, solidly comfortable, unostentatious. An enormous drawing room feels more like a conservatory with high windows opening on two sides, family photos, wood-burner and plenty of sofa space. The dining room, with its large collection of old porcelain to admire, is off to one end; dinners are served with vinho verde, produced from their own grapes down the road. In warmer weather you eat out under the orange trees with views of the hills and the farm's kiwi vines. Big bedrooms are filled with unusual antiques: note the beribboned religious artworks strung between Cor de Rosa's very high beds. Amarelo is perfect for families, as is the lovely new self-catering cottage just down the road. Ask to be shown the unusual paintings in the Quinta's chapel (1623), spin off on their bikes, find time to visit the diminutive castle of nearby Póvoa do Lanhoso. *Minimum two nights.*

Price	€70. House €95-€140. Cottage €80. Prices per night.
Rooms	6 + 2: 6 twins/doubles. House for 2-4. Cottage for 2 + 2 children.
Meals	Dinner with wine, €18. By arrangement. Restaurants a short drive.
Closed	Rarely.
Directions	A3 from Porto, exit Braga Sul & Celeiros. Follow Braga Sul on N103. Left for Amaraes; after 2km left signed Turismo Rural. Signed 'Casa'.

Teresa V Ferreira
Lugar de Portas, Geraz do Minho,
4830-313 Póvoa do Lanhoso

Tel	+351 253 632466
Mobile	+351 964 689970
Email	info@quintasaovicente.com
Web	www.quintasaovicente.com

Quinta do Convento da Franqueira

This 16th-century monastery hides among cork oaks, eucalyptus, cypress and pines. The hugely atmospheric cloisters – sometimes candlelit – are thought to have been built with stones from the ruins of the castle of Faria. Certainly the brothers came here for the peace – and for the spring that now feeds the swimming pool, built above ornamental steps, next to an old font and with fine views of house and church. Five centuries on, the granite buildings have been restored to their former grace by the Gallie family, a labour of love for 'how things were', and the results are delightful. Rooms are generously proportioned and have fine antiques – English and Portuguese. There are old prints, pretty bedside lamps, perhaps a four-poster; the cloisters apartment is a charming hideaway with a terrace and gentle views, the Gatehouse could be a writer's retreat. The estate produces vinho verde and you're nice and close to the sea: the Green Coast is a 20-minute drive. Children have swings in the gardens; grown-ups an honesty bar and lots of books. The village market buzzes on a Thursday – do not miss. *Minimum stay two nights.*

Price	€94–€105. Singles €70. Apartments €560 per week.
Rooms	4 + 2: 2 doubles, 2 twins. Cloiser Flat for 2-3. Gatehouse for 2-3.
Meals	Restaurant 4km.
Closed	November to April.
Directions	A11, exit 3; left to Viana do Csto. 2nd right P. de Varzim. Right under bridge, left to Franqueira. In village, 2nd road uphill to woods & bar. Signed right; left after church.

Piers & Kate Gallie
Carvalhal CC 301,
4755-104 Barcelos

Tel	+351 253 831606
Mobile	+351 962 336622
Email	piers@quintadafranqueira.com
Web	www.quintadafranqueira.com

Quinta de Pindela

You're close to Porto, but it's blissfully quiet. This 80-hectare organic farm, in the family for 600 years, sits in a wide and beautiful valley surrounded by ancient trees. The cottages are hidden well away from each other, and from the 15th-century house where the family lives; arrange to dine in the medieval kitchen. Casa de Soutelo, the largest, is 17th-century, solid and traditional – a typical Minho dwelling built of honey-coloured stone, and facing south. It has big comfortable bedrooms with separate bathrooms, an ample kitchen, a cosy sitting room with an open fire and a long wooden veranda looking down over woods and fields (a perfect spot for lunch). Casa da Bouça, once the farm manager's house, is more contemporary and charming; Casa do Pastor is smaller and simpler. All houses have pools but Bouça's is the most spectacular, built on a giant granite boulder. Your hosts are young people in love with nature, eager that you enjoy life on their farm. Sample Portuguese wines with José, an enologist; go adventuring on horseback (or donkeyback) with Francisco. *Minimum stay one week in summer.*

Price	€75–€140 (€770–€980 per week: high season only).
Rooms	3 cottages: 2 for 4, 1 for 6.
Meals	Dinner €30. Picnic €15. Wine from €12.
Closed	Rarely.
Directions	Exit A3 at Cruz. Left onto N14, right at traffic lights, round cemetary, left down Rua do Vale, keep right into valley.

Maria José Leite-Pereira
Rua de Pindela,
Vila Nova de Famalicão,
4770-130 Cruz, Braga

Mobile	+351 919 062100
Email	turismopindela@live.com.pt
Web	www.quintadepindela.com

Casa de Lamas

Surrounded by cobbled courtyards, manicured gardens and its own private golf course, this solid, formal, 17th-century manor house, complete with 18th-century chapel, breathes Alvim family history and antiquated charm. Rooms are authentically attired: dark wooden antique beds with fabric upholstering and coat-of-arms, period high-backed chairs, grandfather clocks, chandeliers, floral bedspreads and canopy beds, heavy wooden shutters, historical paintings and etchings on the walls – all offset beautifully against white unrendered walls. Self-contained cottages feature curios from previous pastoral incarnations (ploughs, traps, milk urns); black and white marble bathrooms are flawless. After a hard day's exploring Gerês National Park and the vinho verde vineyards, the opulent, book-lined sitting room, artfully cluttered with vases, writing desks, antique weapons and china, provides fabulous aristocratic loafing space, as do the box-hedged and fruit-tree bowered gardens around the lawn-fringed pool. Dine at the new golf club restaurant, or venture out to a family-run joint down the road.

Price	€85–€140.
	Cottages €560–€910 per week.
Rooms	4 + 4: 1 double, 3 twins.
	4 cottages (3 for 2, 1 for 4).
Meals	Dinner with wine, €25.
	By arrangement. Restaurant 500m.
Closed	Never.
Directions	From A7, exit 12 for Arco de Baúlhe; dir. Cabeceiras de Basto. Over N205, follow signs to house, on right just before town.

Miguel Alvim
Lugar de Lamas, Alvite,
4860-333 Cabeceiras de Basto

Tel	+351 253 662202
Mobile	+351 964 273953
Email	info@casadelamas.com
Web	www.smallparadises.pt

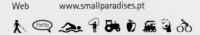

Douro

Residencial Castelo Santa Catarina

This eye-catching building was built high above Porto during the period the Portuguese call the 'Gothic Revival'. You can't fail to be intrigued by this tile-clad, folly-like edifice whose corner turrets and window arches are reminiscent of Notre Dame. It stands surrounded by tall swaying palms in a traditional residential area a metro-ride away from the historic centre, and its wonderful interiors border on the surreal: gilt and stucco, chandeliers and mirrors, cherubs and lozenges, Tiffany lamps and roses, repro beds and cavernous wardrobes. It's showy, over the top, faded in parts, garish in others – great fun. There is ongoing restoration of paintwork, the bathroom colours are often out of step with the rooms and there is no lift to whisk you up and down, but these deficiencies merely add to the charm; the delightful, ever-helpful and multi-lingual João is often around to answer all of your questions. Book the suite in the tower with views, or one of the rooms that opens to the flowery garden, complete with chapel, lounging cats and towering pine tree of twittering birds. Beautiful, characterful, calming.

Price	€75. Singles €60. Suite €95.
Rooms	24: 21 twins/doubles, 3 suites.
Meals	Restaurants nearby.
Closed	Rarely.
Directions	At top of Rua Santa Catarina, just below Plaza Marques Pombal. Follow signs.

	João Brás Rua Santa Catarina 1347, 4000-457 Porto
Tel	+351 225 095599
Email	porto@castelosantacatarina.com.pt
Web	www.castelosantacatarina.com.pt

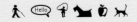

Entry 9   Map 1

Pensão Avenida

Smack bang in the centre of Porto, this wonderfully friendly guest house is run by João Brás and his wife. On the fifth floor of a typical 19th-century townhouse – reached by stairs or lift – are 15 small, plain guest rooms, those at the back overlooking derelict buildings, those at the front with fantastic views over the city. It is, however, good value and feels light, airy, tidy and clean. Enjoy delicious 'pateís de nata' at breakfast in a light-filled breakfast room facing the square and government buildings. This once bohemian area is now filled with trendy clubs, bars and restaurants, some traditional, some modern; Porto is undergoing a culinary renaissance. Your hosts will provide you with all the info and much lies outside the door, including the São Bento train station and the very excellent metro. You can walk to the Torre dos Clérigos, Sé Cathedral, Palácio da Bolsa, Ribeira and the famous Oporto cellars, you can plan a journey up the Douro by boat. No frills, nothing fancy, just a hospitable and well positioned place to lay your head when staying in lovely old Porto.

Price	€45-€50. Singles €35.
Rooms	15: 5 doubles, 8 twins, 2 triples.
Meals	Restaurants nearby.
Closed	Rarely.
Directions	In centre of Porto, opposite Town Hall & São Bento station, near Praça da Liberdade.

João Brás
Avenida dos Aliados 141 4° 5°,
4000-067 Porto
Tel   +351 222 009551
Email   pensaoavenida@clix.pt
Web   pensaoavenida.planetaclix.pt

Casa dos Esteios

In granite farm buildings encircled by organic kiwi plantations are big bedrooms with high ceilings, bountiful breakfasts, ruched white linen and a generous hostess; Maria truly cares for her guests. The wine cellar is now an open-plan living room, the grape press has become a wood-burning stove, and the old stables, set around the courtyard, house those luxurious bedrooms. All feels fresh, bright, uncluttered, spotless, a happy mix of antique and modern. In a sleek, cream fitted kitchen is an old stone bread oven from which smiling Daniella, who was born here, makes tasty breakfasts; enjoy the spread at a big wooden table among English and Portuguese antiques. Wooden floored bedrooms are enlivened by fabrics patterned with English roses and pretty checks; bathrooms are smart-rustic and sparkle. Wake to birdsong, walk to shops and spa, drive to charming old Porto, spin off on a bike, return to a pool with views to the hills and a little play area beautifully maintained. A wonderful place for a group of friends to rent, or to come for a few days' B&B. The peacefulness is the final, blissful treat.

Price	€65–€85. Single €45–€55. Family room €85–€105. Whole house €1,950 per week.
Rooms	6: 2 doubles, 3 twins, 1 family room for 4.
Meals	Restaurants nearby.
Closed	Never.
Directions	From Porto A4 to Penafiel. Exit for Nó de Guilhufe, N106 for 12km. Left to Rio de Moinhos on N312; right signed Casa dos Esteios.

Maria Jorge Nogueira da Rocha
Quinta do Ameal, S. Miguel de Paredes,
4575-371 Penafiel

Tel	+351 962 830700
Mobile	+351 962 830701
Email	nogueirarocha@netcabo.pt
Web	www.casadosesteios.com

Entry 11   Map 1

Casal de Aboadela

Once off the main road you twist and turn along the narrowest of lanes to a sleepy hamlet and this farmhouse. The gardens, magical and meandering, promise a bridged brook, a wood-fired oven, gourds and pumpkins drying in the sun, tables from old millstones, a children's play area, tangerines, oranges, bamboos and vines, and secluded corners for contemplation. The bedrooms are in the main house, simply attired in cottage style with family furniture, and spotless. In a former pigsty to the side is an adorable cottage for two with a kitchen floor of stone and beds that look onto the vines. At the end of the garden, a deliciously contemporary little house for four. The breakfast room is similarly delightful, with its new wooden floor, lovely morning light and great views. Helena and José, wonderful hosts, offer you breakfasts that are generous and delicious, and welcome you on arrival with a bottle of their wine. You can catch the bus to Amarante (for the São Gonçalo monastery – and the internet!), and drive to Braga, Guimarães, Vila Real. There's walking from the door, and a pretty pool to come home to.

Price	€45. Singles €40. Suite €50. Cottage €55. House €60-€120. Prices per night.
Rooms	4 + 2: 3 twins, 1 family suite for 4. Cottage for 2. House for 2-4.
Meals	Picnics & snacks by arrangement. Restaurant 3km.
Closed	Rarely.
Directions	From Amarante, IP4 for Vila Réal. 9km after Amarante, right to Aboadela; signs for 'Turísmo Rural'; right at T-junc.; 'TR' sign to house.

José Silva & Helena Rebelo
Aboadela,
4600-500 Amarante
Tel   +351 255 441141
Mobile   +351 938 469396
Email   srebelo1@gmail.com

Casa da Levada

The crenellated tower is visible as you wind along the cobbled track into this ancient hilltop village, perched high with mountain views. Levada is really a small castle in a settlement built of rough-hewn, moss-covered granite blocks where people and animals still live cheek-by-jowl; Luis's family has been here for 300 years and it's a gem. Rough wooden doors open to reveal a goat, a pair of oxen, the sheaves of corn stacked around a tree trunk to dry: scenes from centuries past. Luis and Maria, she a retired English teacher, are caring hosts with a lively sense of humour. Bedrooms have granite walls, wooden ceilings, beams and sisal floors; the Tower Room has a balcony; the bathroom of the Poet's Room is reached via a trapdoor in the floor! The sitting room is comfortable, the dining room is barn-like, with an oval table at which everyone eats together: the food's delicious, the wine and conversation flow. Find bikes, trampoline, a small pool and a river beach here, and beautiful waterfalls nearby. Up the hill, past the water mills, is a bleak hilltop with great boulders and dolmens – amazing.

Price	€75-€90. Singles €60-€72.
Rooms	5: 1 double, 3 twins; 1 twin with separate bath.
Meals	Dinner, 3 courses with wine, €25. Restaurants 2-15km.
Closed	Rarely.
Directions	From Porto, A4 for Vila Real. After Amarante, exit 18 to Régua. Follow for 8km, then right for Turismo d'habitacão. On for 2km to Travanca do Monte, right, house after 600m.

Luis & Maria Vasconcelos do Lago Mota
Travanca do Monte, Cx. 715, Bustelo,
4600-530 Amarante

Tel	+351 255 433833
Mobile	+351 936 472946
Email	casalevada@clix.pt
Web	www.casalevada.com

Casal Agrícola de Cevêr

Grapes are still crushed by foot in this winery: a labour-intensive process that creates a beautifully soft wine. Here, on the western reaches of the Douro, Alice and her son Filipe produce port, olive oil and a spectacular red. Filipe's tours of the production areas are fascinating and fun (and if you come at the right time, you may join in the harvesting – or the treading!). Guest quarters are comfortable and airy; we liked the suite, lofty, air-conditioned, with embroidered pillow slips and a private gallery. Subtle colour schemes combine with good 19th- and early 20th-century antiques to create a mood of gently old-fashioned calm, there's a sitting room with heaps of books on what to see and do in this lovely green region, a well-equipped kitchen for those wishing to cook, a games room in the basement and a Roman-style swimming pool on its own lawned terrace; enjoy swims to a backdrop of vines. The village of Santa Marta has developed four signposted trails; hiking leaflets are in Portuguese but Filipe can translate. A friendly, unpretentious little place for wine lovers and walkers.

Price	€80. Singles €70. Suites €90. Whole house for 6, €200 (€1,100 per week).
Rooms	4: 1 double, 2 twins, 1 suite.
Meals	Dinner €25, by arrangement.
Closed	Christmas.
Directions	From Porto A4 to Vila Real, exit for Santa Marta de Penaguião onto N2. House signed on right, just before village.

**Filipe Manta Mergulhão &
Alice João Mergulhão**
Quinta do Pinheiro, 5030-569 Sever –
Santa Marta de Penaguião

Tel	+351 254 811274
Mobile	+351 936 884644
Email	casalagricoladecever@casalagricoladecever.com
Web	www.casalagricoladecever.com

Casa d'Além

The cheerful façade of Casa d'Além surveys the stunning terraced vineyards of the Douro valley and reflects the optimism of the early 1920s. The public rooms are the most refined. A Rennie Mackintosh print on sofas and drapes is perfectly balanced by the delicate wrought-iron work of balconies; piano, card table and shining parquet create an atmosphere of old Portugal. Next door is a panelled dining room for sociable meals and a remarkable, long, hand-painted corridor, a 'marbled sunburst', that leads to the rooms. Discover a feast of period pieces: rugs, marble-topped dressers and vast vintage tubs and washstands. No TVs encourages conviviality, and every room has a heavenly view. Paulo and his wife speak excellent English and their marvellous staff take care of you; ask Elisabete about customised trips along the Douro – by boat or steam train – and do visit the Mateus Palace in Vila Réal. Outside are beautifully maintained grounds, hilltop air, a secluded infinity pool. Don't miss dinner: perhaps a roast from their bread oven, homemade ice-cream, a local wine. It's a treat.

Price	€80. Singles €70. Family room €85-€100.
Rooms	3: 1 double, 1 twin, 1 family room.
Meals	Lunch & dinner, 3 courses with wine, from €20. Light meals €8.
Closed	Rarely.
Directions	From Porto A4 for Vila Real; N101 to Mesão Frio. Continue 8km to Granjão. Under bridge; left to Oliveira; signed on left. Do not confuse with Oliveira on other side of river.

Paulo José F S Dias Pinheiro
Oliveira,
5040-204 Mesão Frio

Tel	+351 254 321991
Email	casadalem@sapo.pt
Web	www.casadalem.pt

Casa de Vilarinho de São Romão

An old place with a young heart. The 17th-century house at the end of the tree-lined, gated drive overlooks the Pinhão valley; the atmospheric chapel at the entrance is even older. Inside find warm sunny colours, light, elegance and space. Cristina gave up teaching to concentrate on the house, and later turned her attention to the vineyards; her Dutch-Portuguese ancestors are a port-wine family. All is harmony and light: white walls, polished kilim-strewn floors, grand paintings, fine antiques. One bedroom has twin brass beds and granite window seats, another an ornately carved bed, all have long drapes and immaculate bathrooms, some with walk-in showers. The sitting room has a beautiful octagonal 'maçeira' ceiling and a cosy fire for winter; outside are a shaded terrace where you breakfast in summer on fresh juices and fruits from the farm. Traditional dinners sound tempting. There's much to enjoy: the inner gravelled courtyard with dolphin-spouting fountains, the serene pool, the walks through the vineyards and, always, those long, long views across the Pinhão valley.

Price	€85. Singles €70. Extra bed €20.
Rooms	6: 2 doubles, 4 twins.
Meals	Dinner €25, by arrangement.
Closed	Christmas.
Directions	From Vila Real to Pinhão through Sabrosa; in Vilarinho de São Romão, you will see a green wooden gateway & chapel on left. Through gate.

Cristina van Zeller
Lugar da Capela, Vilarinho de
São Romão, 5060-630 Sabrosa

Tel   +351 259 930754
Email   mail@casadevilarinho.com
Web   www.casadevilarinho.com

Casa de Casal de Loivos

The view is amazing and every room opens to it. This village manor house, home to the Sampaios since 1733, sits high above the mightly Douro. Tradition, comfort and gentility are the hallmarks here. Charming Manuel is a gentleman of the old school, and attracts a cultivated clientele; he speaks perfect English, sports a cravat and likes you to dress up for dinner. Delicious traditional dishes from old family recipes are served in a beautiful dining room at a perfectly dressed table: dinner is a convivial affair. Breakfasts are out on the terrace, a feast of home produce including juice from blood oranges and their own lemonade. A sitting room opens to terrace, small garden and pool, while the vineyard below can be strolled at leisure. View-filled bedrooms are elegant, gorgeous, with smart bathrooms and servants' bells – order an aperitif and a bowl of roasted almonds! Fuelled by good food and wine, bewitched by the interplay of light, land and water, pampered by Manuel and his courteous staff, gourmets, wine lovers and walkers not adverse to a dash of class will be in heaven.

Price	€100. Singles €80.
Rooms	6: 3 doubles, 3 twins.
Meals	Dinner €25, by arrangement. Wine €10-€50.
Closed	24-25 December & January.
Directions	From Pinhão to Alijó; 1st right & up through vineyards until Casal de Loivos. House on right at end of village.

Manuel Bernardo de Sampaio
Casal de Loivos,
5085-010 Pinhão

Tel	+351 254 732149
Email	casadecasaldeloivos@ip.pt
Web	www.casadecasaldeloivos.com

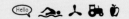

Casa do Visconde de Chanceleiros

Lie in the lap of Douro luxury. Delicious big beds, thick fluffy towels, generous hosts, happy staff, a dining terrace with a panorama… and Molly, the mascot bulldog, never short of a cuddle. Kurt and Ursula's home is a classic manor house on the edge of a hillside village, with vine-covered terraces to one side and stunning views over valley and river. Wide granite steps lead down to a huge pool with a long-roofed cabana furnished with sofa, music and tables; there are wrought-iron sunbeds with plump cushions, a sauna in a port barrel (wonderful), metal racehorses on the lawn, lush flowers, an outdoor jacuzzi. All is tasteful, stylish, informal yet not over-casual. Indoors, strong warm colours are set off by terracotta, granite and slate and an inviting mix of contemporary and antique. Bedrooms are a very good size; one is on two floors, ideal for a family; all have delightful bathrooms and hand-painted furniture. Ursula, who loves to bring people together, may join you at dinner; the food is a treat. All this and masses to do: ping-pong, tennis, squash, billiards and boules here, hiking and biking beyond.

Price	€130. Family room €165. Suite €145.
Rooms	10: 5 doubles, 1 family room, 4 suites.
Meals	Lunch & dinner with wine, €35. By arrangement.
Closed	Rarely.
Directions	A4 from Porto to Vila Real; exit for Chaves. At r'bout follow signs to Sabrosa; then turn for Pinhão. There, follow signs for Chanceleiros.

Kurt & Ursula Böcking
Largo da Fonte,
Chanceleiros-Covas do Douro,
5085-201 Pinhão

Tel	+351 254 730190
Email	chanceleiros@chanceleiros.com
Web	www.chanceleiros.com

Casas do Côro

Minimalist modern houses are scattered throughout the grounds, dramatically embedded in the hugely atmospheric medieval village of Marialva with terraces and towers overlooking the garden and sun-decked, umbrella-lined pool — and cotton-swathed day bed. Ancient battlements creep uphill between olive and almond trees; views reach across vines, whitewashed, red-roofed village and imposing castle to shrub-covered hills. A lavish, theatrical feel prevails; rooms are opulently decorated, with fancy fittings, modern art, embroidered linen, bedspreads and rugs made by Paulo's factory, silk curtains, printed wallpaper, masses of birch panelling, sleek spoiling bathrooms and more cushions than you'll ever need; immaculate, tasteful, considered. The main house salon, equally impeccable, has a marvellous fireplace, wooden parquet, honesty bar, deep sofas, incense and plenty of reading material. The food is modern regional and you dine regally beneath a huge chandelier gazing out past granite pillars to panoramic views. It's child-friendly, and there's masses to see and do in these history-steeped environs. *A Rusticae property.*

Price	€125-€175. Suites €240-€280. Houses €185-€840. All prices per night.
Rooms	6 + 7: 4 doubles, 1 single, 1 suite. 7 houses: 1 for 2, 2 for 4, 2 for 5, 1 for 6, 1 for 6-8.
Meals	Dinner with wine, €55, by arrangement.
Closed	Never.
Directions	From Porto, A1 for Aveiro, exit 16, A25 to Viseu, at Celorico da Beira exit on IP2 for Foz da Côa, exit to Marialva. Thro' village, signed.

Paulo Romão
Marialvamed - Turismo Histórico
e Lazer Lda, Apartado 1,
6430-081 Marialva

Tel	+351 917 552020
Email	info@casasdocoro.com.pt
Web	www.casasdocoro.com.pt

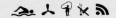

Entry 19   Map 2

Quinta Souto Covo

Wind through the forest to discover an 18th-century, split-level house with hand-cut slate roofs and vine-smothered walls. The two suites are cosy, comfortable and inviting, with white walls, old beams and clever contemporary touches. The Lodge comes with an African themed sitting room (Moroccan furniture, big game paintings), its mezzanine bedroom and balcony sharing superlative sylvan views; as your extrovert host says, "nobody has ever closed the curtains." It's a painter's paradise (Picasso apparently stayed). Outside, terraces cascade to the tinkling river, with productive vines, natural spring pool below, a riverside 'beach' swimming area with sun terrace, hammocks and benches strewn about, a huge fig tree, a wildflower meadow, little details like gargoyles and granite feed troughs, trees galore (chestnuts, cherry, quince, hazel, walnut, oaks), and pet rabbits, goldfish and dogs. An organic veg patch provides for Thai/Italian meals; Sherrin is an excellent and imaginative cook. Fly-fish trout for supper, birdwatch for Bonelli eagles, kingfishers, hoopoes, and explore the woods with a picnic. Bliss.

Price	€90. Child €10–€30. Lodge €129–€159. All prices per night.
Rooms	3 + 1: 1 single, 2 suites for 2-4. Lodge for 7.
Meals	Dinner, with wine, €19. Restaurant 5-minute drive.
Closed	Mid-January to mid-March.
Directions	A24 to Castro Daire Leste; down to Ponte Pedrenha. Right for S.P. do Sul, right to Reriz. Thro' town to Ponte Cabaços, back on yourself uphill for 400m, on left.

Sherrin Cottrell
3600-604 Reriz

Tel	+351 232 382794
Mobile	+351 914 234323
Email	sherrincottrell@hotmail.com
Web	www.quintasoutocovo.com

Beira

Casa Campo das Bizarras

Pootle through the apple orchard to the fine old granite farmhouse where a corner of old Portugal has been lovingly preserved. Both house and hamlet have bags of character: heavy oak beams, stone floors, and a wonderfully atmospheric bar in the cobbled cellar (try the apple brandy). There's a delightful reading room and a drawing room crammed with family treasures. The long low kitchen has a large inglenook, a bread oven and a marble-topped table for breakfast; here you plan your day's excursions with friendly Marina – this is a hugely historic region. Bedrooms in the main house and wing have dark antiques and curtains edged with the regional lace; some have private bathrooms across the corridor. Apartments, three rustic (one with a vine growing though!), one invitingly modern, have simple kitchenettes, but there's a communal kitchen plus two barbecues. A pretty raised pool with Roman steps, basketball, darts, and a play area provide further entertainment. The garden is lovely, with its hammocks, peacocks and secret corners. You can hear the hum from the A24 below but the value is hard to beat.

Price	€56-€70. Singles €45-€55. Apt for 2, €70-€87 (€425-€525 p.w.). Apt for 4, €87-€120 (€525-€725 p.w.).
Rooms	5 + 4: 4 doubles, 1 twin, some with separate baths. 4 apts: 3 for 2-4, 1 for 2-5.
Meals	Restaurant 10-minute walk.
Closed	Rarely.
Directions	From Castro Daire to Fareja. In Fareja left at sign for 'Turísmo Rural'. Past church, up narrow cobbled lane, Bizarras on right.

Marina Rodrigues Moutinho
Rua da Capela 76, Fareja,
3600-271 Castro Daire

Tel	+351 232 386107
Mobile	+351 962 709988
Email	casa@campodasbizarras.com
Web	www.campodasbizarras.com

Quinta da Vila Francelina

Tall and stately, this dazzling 1909 house from the Art Nouveau era hangs above the Rio Vouga. Views sweep from the pool across the extraordinary bird- and willow-strewn *pateira* (water meadow) that leads to the Aveira lagoon, 17 kilometres down the coast. The landscape is reflected in this most gracious house, whose walls and ceilings are hand-painted with charming scenes of rivers and wildlife. António and Maria's home is immaculate inside. Light airy bedrooms are elegant with grand polished bedheads, tall windows and exquisite decorative touches; the room under the eaves has inspirational views. The annexe rooms, one in the old dovecote, are, in contrast, urban and contemporary: expect bold paintings on white walls, rugs on polished floors, sleek lighting and super big bathrooms. There's plenty of space here to unwind: in the library or the delightful games room (ping-pong, snooker), on the court or by the saltwater pool. Children have gardens to explore and beaches nearby. Walk in the pine and eucalyptus forest, take a boat trip through the dreamy water meadows, pop into the village. Wonderful.

Price	€85. Singles €75.
Rooms	10: 3 doubles. 7 doubles in annexe.
Meals	Lunch & dinner €25. Kitchens on request.
Closed	Rarely.
Directions	From A1 exit 16 for Aveiro norte, onto A25; exit 6 for Angeja. Left after 2km for Frossos/S.João de Loure. Quinta 3km on left.

António Pinho
Vila Francelina Frossos,
Albergaria-a-Velha, 3850-663 Aveiro

Tel +351 917 203471
Mobile +351 917 203471
Email info@quintadavilafrancelina.pt
Web www.quintadavilafrancelina.pt

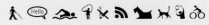

Casa do Sol Nascente

'The house of the rising sun' sits in an uncommonly lush corner of Portugal; guests come for the welcome and the peace. Enter a column of glass around which curves a flight of stairs; the architecture is the work of Japanese Chizu, whose paintings hang in the rooms. Comfortable downstairs bedrooms have white walls and polished dark furniture, but the best room is the upstairs suite, with a private terrace and a jacuzzi. Gentle Chizu and Ian are welcoming and well-travelled, as easy with city escapees as with young families; the mood is very relaxed. The garden, running down to the river, is large and lush with figs, persimmons and fruit trees; Ian also grows shitake mushrooms. Meals from Chizu are superb and span a wide range of Portuguese and Japanese dishes, vegetarian included; in summer you can enjoy barbecues under the bamboo pergola resplendent with vines and kiwi. Nearby are the gorgeous bird-rich Aveiro lagoons, sand beaches are five miles away, and you can ride on horseback to the watery Ria. You don't need a car to get here: the public transport is excellent. *Ask about meditation weekends.*

Price	€45. Suite €78. Apt €930 per week.
Rooms	4 + 1 : 2 doubles/twins, 2 suites. Apartment for 6.
Meals	Lunch & dinner, à la carte, from €18. By arrangement.
Closed	Rarely.
Directions	A1; N235 for Aveiro; immed. right to Mamodeiro; at café, right to Requeixo. On to Taipa. Road bends to right; at bend take smaller road up to right; last house, 800m.

Ian M Arbuckle
Rua da Alagoa, Taipa, Requeixo,
3800-881 Aveiro

Tel	+351 234 933597
Mobile	+351 966 014248
Email	arbuckle@mail.telepac.pt
Web	www.solnascente.aveiro.co.pt

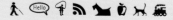

Quinta dos Três Rios

This large mid-19th-century granite house is pervaded by a generous spirit: Hugh's boyish enthusiasm and Jane's motherly pragmatism. High-ceilinged and ultra-comfortable ground-floor suites are bright and beautiful with fabulous antiques and views; the more modern but still characterful upstairs suites show off a tangle of beams. Stylish local black pottery is for sale in the breakfast room, where garden raspberries, the owners' own eggs and home-made stewed fruit compote kickstart the day. A fantastic-value dinner is taken en famille around the large table or on the terrace between the fairy lights, perhaps smoked salmon with cucumber and tarragon salad, chicken piri-piri, lemon posset. Count shooting stars in August or help tread the grapes at the end of September/early October. Honeymooners might enjoy a candlelit dinner in the vineyard, while solo travellers are folded into the embrace of this convivial place. Nearby, a river beach and thermal springs beckon, up the hill a flash new restaurant is set to open. The friendly village is down the road, and there's a cycle track to boot. Perfection!

Price	€85–€125. Family suite €135–€165.
Rooms	6: 4 suites, 2 family suites for 4.
Meals	Dinner, 3 courses with wine, €20. Packed lunch €10–€15. Restaurant 4km.
Closed	Never.
Directions	Exit IP3 for Parada de Gonta, right at 1st junction, up hill & down through village. Entrance gates on right after sharp left with chevrons.

Hugh & Jane Forestier-Walker
Rua Francisco de Oliveira 239,
Parada de Gonta, 3460-391 Tondela
Tel +351 232 959189
Mobile +351 916 684484
Email hugh.jane@minola.co.uk
Web www.minola.co.uk

Entry 24 Map 1

Quinta do Rio Dão

The river setting is a dream: the house hides in a stand of old oaks on the banks of a small lagoon. Dutch owners Pieter and Juliette live here with their sons – brought up on the farmstead when it still stood in ruins – and have sensitively restored it in traditional Beira style. They are excellent, multi-lingual hosts, and give you the choice of B&B in their house or self-catering in the apartments and cottages. In four well set-apart *casas*, (some old and some new), a traditional Portuguese look marries with an uncluttered space; nothing fancy, nothing to distract you from the beauty of the place. Bedrooms are not large but have a sunny feel; bathrooms are modern; and there are verandas aplenty for captivating views down to the river. In summer, life is spent mostly outdoors: birdsong at breakfast; at night, the lights of Santa Comba Dão twinkling across the water. There are canoes and a rowing boat to borrow, a pool to share and mountain bikes to rent: you are at the start of a 55km eco path. The feel is of a mini holiday village, it's good value and now there's horse riding, too. *Minimum stay two nights.*

Price	€65-€75. Cottage for 2-4, €65-€135. Cottage for 5-8, €170-€205. Prices per night.
Rooms	2 + 4: 1 double, 1 triple. 4 cottages: 2 for 2-4, 2 for 5-8.
Meals	Breakfast for self-caterers €7. Restaurants 5-10km.
Closed	Rarely.
Directions	From Lisbon, A1 for Porto. After Coimbra, IP3 for Viseu. 500m before Sta Comba Dão, to Vimieiro. Signed Agro Turismo, 4.5km to Quinta.

Pieter & Juliette Gruppelaar-Spierings
3440-464 Santa Comba Dão

Tel	+351 232 892784
Email	quinta2@quintadoriodao.com
Web	www.quintadoriodao.com

Casa de Santa Ana da Beira

You could be staying in a Portuguese relative's home: expect a family welcome and delicious home cooking. Joaquim's generations-old family house stands by the village church near Portugal's highest peaks; he and Maria Laura (who speaks excellent English) left Lisbon for rural tranquillity. Gambol in the garden between citrus, peaches and figs, or set kids loose on the swings; there's a pool, tennis court, pergolas and, for a small fee, a covered open-air whirlpool. Inside is replete with antiques, lace, oil paintings, ceramics, the family coat-of-arms on a dark blue felt curtain, a wine adega… even the games room holds antiques. Lower ground-floor bedrooms, off the garden, continue the traditional theme: no frills, just comfortable, generous, with carved headboards and beautifully patterned fabrics. Breakfast on homemade jams and local cheese on the terrace or in the wood-panelled, fire-warmed dining room. Lunch – served in the new glass-fronted garden room – is cooked with their own olive oil. Serra da Estrela is a playground of trails, museums, village festivals and, in winter, snowboarding.

Price	€64–€68.
Rooms	5: 2 doubles, 2 twins; 1 triple sharing bathroom.
Meals	Lunch & dinner €15. Wine €8–€15. Restaurant 3km.
Closed	24 December.
Directions	From IP3, exit at Rojão Grande onto IC12 dir. Mangualde. In Nelas centre, at r'bout dir. Seia onto N231. After 12km, left in Paranhos onto R. Luciano Homem Ferreira.

	Joaquim & Laura Homem Ferreira Rua Luciano Homem Ferreira 11, 6270-133 Paranhos da Beira
Tel	+351 238 976161
Email	ter@csadabeira.com
Web	www.casadesantaanadabeira.com

Dominio Vale do Mondego

A river valley retreat with an air of creativity: artwork and sculptures framed against the majestic Serra de Estrela. Sculpt, paint, or sit and daydream in the atelier. You can do it all here: B&B in the cosy cabanas with comfy beds, old beams, granite boulders and simple bathroom; self-cater in the country-style quintas (exposed walls, colourful tiles, modern touches – one house has its own pool); or camp in isolated bliss. Dutch owners Karin and Eelco, a generous pair, encourage a communal vibe amongst their 33 heavenly hectares of olive groves, veg gardens, pastures, woodland and orchards. Farming organically for over 30 years, the family work the land, care for their sheep, make cheese and press olive oil using biodynamic practices. Ice-cold water comes from the spring and they are completely self-sufficient for energy. Buy your basics from the farmshop or eat a divine home-cooked meal in the convivial Lagar Lounge – or in the shade of a fig tree. There are horses to gallop and donkeys to plod. Hike in the park, swim in the shared pool, and don't miss the arts festival they host every August.

Price	€35-€55. Houses €315-€1,450 per week.
Rooms	3 + 3: 2 doubles; 1 single sharing bath. 3 houses: 1 for 9, 1 for 4, 1 for 3-4. 4 tents in grounds.
Meals	Breakfast for self-caterers €5. Dinner €15. Wine €5. Restaurant 12km.
Closed	B&B & tents closed October to May.
Directions	From Viseu A25 dir. Guarda; exit 28 to Porto da Carne. 5km to Faia. Thro' village on new road; on exiting, by angel sculpture, on right.

Karin Sligting
Quinta da Portela,
6300-095 Faia

Tel	+351 271 926276
Mobile	+351 938 750730
Email	info@dominiovaledomondego.com
Web	www.dominiovaledomondego.com

Casa das Penhas Douradas Design Hotel

Snake 1,500m up a winding pass to the 'first mountain resort in Portugal.' The surrounding hamlet is 120 years old but the hotel is new: all clean lines, blonde wood and touches of colour in locally made felt rugs and stool covers. Everywhere there are vintage wooden skis set off by funky 50s style lamps. Chalet-style bedrooms, some with balconies, all with stunning views to river valleys, are cool and calming with spotless, state-of-the-art bathrooms. Dinner is a gourmet affair in the gleaming dining room (open for non-residents too) followed by a gentle stroll to a quartz outcrop: you're in the Serra da Estrela Natural Park and its wooded, boulder-strewn hills; note the Penhas Douradas gleaming golden in the setting sun. João, your ever-helpful host, can point you in the direction of gentle walking trails and challenging hikes, or kayaking round the nearby lake. Return to a library stuffed with books and DVDs, a sitting room with a fireplace to curl up in front of, a delicious spa and a pool with floor-to-ceiling windows. Gulp in the restorative air, wonder at the huge skies – it's stunning.

Price	€90–€135. Singles €75–€120. Suite €180–€220.
Rooms	18: 8 doubles, 9 twins, 1 suite.
Meals	Lunch €20. Dinner €30. Wine included. Packed lunch €10. Restaurant 13km.
Closed	Never.
Directions	From Porto A1 south, A25 until Mangualde, N232 towards Manteigas.

	João Tomás
	Apartado 9,
	6260-200 Manteigas
Tel	+351 275 981045
Email	mail@casadaspenhasdouradas.pt
Web	www.casadaspenhasdouradas.pt

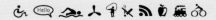

Entry 28   Map 1

Casas da Lapa

In the steepest village of the Serra da Estrela (lots of goats, two small cafés) hides this über-trendy, eco-style guest house. 'Lapa' means 'large rock': great granite boulders lie at the core of the 19th-century house. Bright and funky is the décor, luxurious are the bathrooms, with pampering hydromassage tubs, while bedrooms deliver striking bold colours, underfloor heating and incense if you'd like it. Sensational views stretch across serene rural landscapes and the veranda is a perfect platform for sunsets. Tuck into an impressive selection of breakfast cheeses: Serra, Azores, Portuguese brie; at weekends, juices, scrambled eggs and sausages are added to your plate. Dinner is delicious contemporary Portuguese, accompanied by a sparkling wine made by Maria's parents. Hill walking is big here, natural reservoirs abound and Portugal's highest peak (with skiing at Torre) isn't far; Nuno will eagerly show you the way if he's around. Or be a lazybones and loll by the pool to the background trickle of the waterfall. Attentive staff look after your every whim. *Two self-catering apartments close by.*

Price	€90–€115. Singles €75–€100. Extra bed €20.
Rooms	8: 6 doubles, 2 twins.
Meals	Lunch €12. Dinner, 2 courses with wine, €25. Restaurants 7km.
Closed	24-25 December.
Directions	From Porto, A1 to A25, dir. Viseu, exit 18 onto N231 dir. Nelas; to São Romão, then continue on N231 4km past Parque Natural Serra de Estrela sign; 1st left; signed.

Nuno & Maria Manuel
Rua da Eira de Costa 10,
Lapa dos Dinheiros, 6270-651 Seia

Tel	+351 934 560401
Email	info@casasdalapa.com
Web	www.casasdalapa.com

Quinta da Moenda

Life is unhurried here. Donkeys pull carts, sheep meander through villages and the bakery is the top place in town. Tucked between the Açor and Estrela mountains, above the river Alvoco, the quinta has a timeless feel that Dutch owners Hans and Josephine have done little to disturb. An 18th-century water mill and olive mill make up their home, and the distillery has been converted into apartments. Compact and unfussy, they are furnished with modern pine and terracotta, bright beds, sofabeds and curtains, wood-burners, perhaps a veranda with a mountain view; one lies by the patio so you can sit in the sun as the children snooze. Walk through pine and eucalyptus forests, canoe and swim in the river; in winter there's skiing in the Serra da Estrela. Spot otters on the lovely riverside walk to the village, return to a pretty pergola and a fenced pool, raise your glass to the stars with only the rush of the river to disturb the peace. There's a communal living space and a lovely big patio surrounded by hollyhocks and hydrangeas, with a summer kitchen and a barbecue, too. And a sauna is on its way.

Price	€75 for 2. Extra bed €22.50. Prices per night. Under 4s free.
Rooms	5 apartments for 2-4.
Meals	Welcome hamper €30. Summer kitchen. Restaurant 10-minute drive.
Closed	Rarely.
Directions	From Coimbra IP3 dir. Viseu; IC6 to exit 9, right; at r'bout left to Oliveira do H.; at Vendas de G. right; at Ponte das T.E. left on bridge, Alvoco das Várzeas 4km. Signed.

Josephine van Bennekom &
Hans de Herder
Avenida da Fronteira, Alvoco das Várzeas,
3400-301 Oliveira do Hospital

Tel	+351 238 666443/mobile +351 961 337611
Email	quintadamoenda@gmail.com
Web	www.quintadamoenda.com

Entry 30   Map 1

Casa do Castelo Novo

The garden is simple, flourishing, the views are wonderful and the whole place is, according to one reader, "a joy." The Casa is a 17th-century home on the slopes of the Serra da Gardunha, an amphitheatre that drops to the impossibly narrow streets of a hilltop village; it is blissfully peaceful. The granite front of this elegant casa is deceptive: you cannot guess how the house is built up the steep rock, nor that the garden is at the level of the first floor. The ground floor is a guest sitting room, with sofas, a wall of rock, carpets from Morocco. Up a wooden staircase is the main living room; more sofas, a granite fireplace, a Maceira ceiling, bookcases cut into the walls, clay figures, modern lithographs, fine china. Feast-like breakfasts are served in a Victorian-parlour style dining room. Above the sitting room is the two-storey suite, with Dona Maria beds and the best view in the house. A few steps across the garden are a painted Alentejan triple and a romantic twin; bathrooms are simple. Delightful Alice and Manuel help you organise jeep or bike tours, guided walks and serve you superb Portuguese food.

Price	€65. Singles €50. Suite €75.
Rooms	4: 1 twin, 1 suite for 4. Annexe: 1 twin, 1 triple.
Meals	Dinner with wine, €20-€25. By arrangement.
Closed	Rarely.
Directions	A23 to Fundão. 10km south of Fundão, exit for Castelo Novo. Enter on R. de São Brãs; at Largo da Bica right along R. da Gardunha, round castle; signed.

Alice Aleixo
Rua Nossa Senhora das Graças 7,
6230-160 Castelo Novo

Tel	+351 275 561373
Mobile	+351 919 636032
Email	castelo.novo@gmail.com
Web	www.castelonovo.web.pt

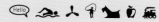

Casa Tejo

Bliss to laze on the roof terrace and gaze on the Tejo Valley, in the lush countryside of the Alto Alentejo. You are immersed in old Portugal here, on the edge of a village set in time; this charming house, a barn and farm cottage combined, is the restoration of owners Lise and Udo who live nearby and entertain in their wine cellar. Step in to find old beams, rough-rendered walls, a magnificent chestnut table with hand-carved chairs, sofas with throws and a friendly log fire. At the top of hand-painted terracotta stairs is the roof terrace, accessible from a galleried double bedroom in the old fruit loft. The second bedroom, a spacious twin, has a balcony over a garden pretty with vines, fruit trees, an ancient olive – and views. Through the pergola, the final treat: a walled courtyard with a barbecue and pool. The area, 'Portugal's Provence', is loved by artists, walkers and nature lovers; waterfalls and river beaches abound and the bird life is amazing. The gentle climate makes this a sweet spot for an out of season stay – if you come in November you can watch the olives being harvested. *Min. three nights.*

Price	€60–€75 (€250–€475 p.w.).
Rooms	House for 4-6 (1 double, 1 twin; sofabed).
Meals	Restaurant 4km.
Closed	Rarely.
Directions	A23, exit 16 signed Riscada-Juncal; under dual c'way; left at T-junc. for Silveira. Pass/turn to Riscada & continue thro' tunnel to Silveira. In village, follow road to right; past bread oven & fountain.

Udo & Lise Reppin
Monte da Portelinha, Silveira,
6030-021 Fratel

Tel	+351 274 822303
Mobile	+351 918 937889
Email	lidoreppin@hotmail.com
Web	www.udoandlisereppin.com

Entry 32   Map 4

Moinho da Meia Lua

Welcome to the highest habitation in the province! The forest is behind… before you, enormous views reach to the Alentejo and Spain. Charming Lise and Udo live in an edge-of-village house between two tracks, with a secluded terraced garden they lovingly tend and an emerald rectangle of a pool, yours to share. You live in the luxurious little cabana behind, with a cosy living room, a bedroom in the loft, and a fabulous terrace with a natural stone table. All is simple, restful, contemporary, with hand-crafted furniture, knitted throws and Moroccan/Mexican touches; ceiling fans and aircon for summer, wood-burner for winter, delicious soaps by the shower. Life is lived in the slow lane here, in a world almost untouched by the 21st century: donkeys work in the fields, goats graze. Your hosts are friendly people with a strong sense of style; they give you delicious breakfasts in the summer kitchen, and dinner in their adega; they know and love the area, and will tell you all you need to know. Yours to discover are the village restaurants, bars, little shops and blissful river beach. *Minimum two nights.*

Price	€40-€80.
Rooms	Cabana for 2.
Meals	Dinner with wine, €15-€30. By arrangement.
Closed	Rarely.
Directions	From A23, exit 18 for Serta on N241. After Moitas, right for Oleiras N351; after 10km left to Vale da Ursa. Thro' Ribeira, then in Vale da Ursa right into square, then right up steep road, house after 30m.

Udo & Lise Reppin
Rua Alta, Vale da Ursa,
6150-740 Sobreira Formosa

Tel	+351 274 822303
Mobile	+351 918 937889
Email	lidoreppin@hotmail.com
Web	www.udoandlisereppin.com

Entry 33   Map 4

Yurt Holiday Portugal

You're deep in nature but can still have a cold beer and hot shower. That's the idea behind the McDonnells' glamping spot among the Schist villages — a slice of wild-and-wonderful with all the trimmings. Two yurts appear in the garden when spring flowers peep: a mimosa wood mesh topped by wool rugs and tarpaulin, spiked with a skylight, fitted with bright double beds, armchairs and nifty terracotta drinks coolers. Your living space extends into a garden of figs, olives, vines, fruit trees, fresh herbs, a burbling brook… perfect for badminton, croquet or lazing in the hammock. Bathrooms are private and close by, with hot showers, handmade soaps and composting loos; all is solar-powered apart from the showers. Derek and Hannah are dynamic ex-Londoners with two lovely kids and dog Baloo, chickens too; both are passionate about the environment. They bring dinners to your yurt and fresh milk from town; breakfast arrives in a basket under the sweet chestnut. The sleepy surroundings hide river beaches, hiking trails through cork forests, horse riding, restaurants and wine farms. Kooky, fun, fabulous. *Minimum two nights.*

Price	€65-€80 for 2 (€400-€490 p.w.). Bell tent/yurt pod €50-€60 per week.
Rooms	2 yurts for 2-4. Bell tent & yurt pod with 2 child's beds.
Meals	Dinner with wine, €13.50 & €19.
Closed	October to April.
Directions	From Porto A29 south; exit IP3 for Guarda; exit 13 to IP6, thro' Arganil. Right at r'bout by fountain, right at r'bout for Gois. Left at chapel, 6km; past Pracerias, on right.

Derek & Hannah McDonnell
Lugar Varzeas, Pracerias,
3300-207 Arganil

Tel	+351 235 208562
Email	yurtholidayportugal@gmail.com
Web	www.yurtholidayportugal.com

Casa da Palmira

If you're looking for a small comfortable perch in the Serra da Lousã, head here. In a newly restored building in the centre of town, on a corner with lots of windows, is an apartment above and offices below – plus covered internal parking (a boon) and a simple furnished patio near the bays. The kitchen is well-equipped with a quasi-country feel, bedrooms have fans and the bathroom is lovely with plants, tub, shower and an old dresser that Carlos, the friendly owner/builder, restored to take a basin. Floors are new pine made to look antique, paintwork is distressed, tiles are pristine, walls are yellows and blues, and all feels light, airy, friendly and cute. The town is big enough to house bars, restaurants and cafés, there's a castle with a natural swimming pool and the wonderful Serra da Lousã is on the doorstep. Sites of special beauty include the Mata do Sobral and the São João valley: pull on your hiking boots! Note too the river beach at Gois, the Roman ruins at Conimbriga, and the historic university town of Coimbra – you can see them all in a day. *Minimum two nights.*

Price	€85 (€550 per week).
Rooms	Apartment for 4.
Meals	Restaurants 5-minute walk.
Closed	Never.
Directions	From Coimbra, N17, then N236 dir. Lousã, thro' town past station, right at first hairpin, onto R. Dr. Francisco Viana, number 27.

Carlos Martins
R. Dr. Francisco Viana 27,
3200-380 Lousã

Mobile	+351 916 705774
Email	carlos@historicholidayportugal.com
Web	www.historicholidayportugal.com

Casa da Azenha Velha

The old *azenha* (flour mill) has changed a fair bit, though decorative flourishes above doors and large rooms suggest a grand history. Bedrooms, away from the house, all a good size, surround a pretty garden and flowers grow up around your windows. Furnishings are basic: big beds have old-fashioned bedcovers and there's a mini fridge for each room. Pamper yourself with a soak in big tubs – ideal for children! Delightful Maria serves you breakfast in the kitchen of the main house, where Portuguese pottery and old farm implements decorate high walls – all the way up to the ceiling. A sitting room in the stable block has an honesty bar, comfy sofas, an open fire and board games; outside are a big pool, a tennis court, a snooker table and a barbecue. A short walk through the fields brings you to the family's attractively rustic restaurant, for regional and international dishes. Children can make friends with Maria's dog, sheep and horse, experienced riders may have a ride, and the mood is nicely relaxed; this is a good place for young families and groups. Great value.

Price	€80. Triple €100. Singles €65. Apartment €115 per night.
Rooms	6 + 1: 3 doubles, 3 triples. Apartment for 2-4.
Meals	Dinner from €10. Wine €4.50. Not Mondays.
Closed	Rarely.
Directions	From A1 exit onto A14 dir. Figuiera da Foz. Exit A14 for Caceira; immed. left signed Turismo Rural. After 2km, right; 500m, right. On left.

Maria de Lourdes Nogueira
Caceira de Cima, 3080-399
Figueira da Foz

Mobile	+351 914 607493
Email	casaazenhavelha@hotmail.com
Web	www.azenhavelha.no.comunidades.net

Estremadura & Ribatejo

The House of the She-Pine-Tree

Artistic flair: this historic museum-house has it in palette-fuls, from its balconied terracota façade to the explosion of Portuguese Modernist art within. Covering every inch of wall are the bold oil paintings, pastels and sketches of Olavo d'Eça Leal, a prolific, bohemian, sometimes scandalous artist, a journalist, author and public figure – and grandfather of adventurous, multi-lingual owners Duarte and Bernardo. Hear their stories over a cocktail from the honesty bar or dinner (it's brilliant value); shoot the breeze on a patio shaded by the eponymous pine, cool off in the new pool, retire to bedrooms swimming with art, colour and eccentricity. Ornate bedsteads, old chests, shutters, balconies, quirky bathrooms… Olavo's desk in one, his gun collection and typewriter in another. (Not for minimalists and, note, two bedrooms are on the lower ground floor.) The peaceful village flaunts a 280-year-old fountain that made its washerwomen famous, and views that catapult towards the world heritage town of Sintra and the valley's pink marble quarries: there are adventures to be had. Seductive, unique, inspired.

Price	€65-€120. Chapel House €55-€100 per night.
Rooms	8 + 1: 4 suites, 1 suite for 4; 2 doubles sharing bath, 1 double with separate bath. Chapel House for 6.
Meals	Dinner, 3 courses, €11. Packed lunch €7.50. Wine €6-€15. Restaurant 150m.
Closed	Never.
Directions	A5 for Cascais; exit 6, Crel; exit 2A Sintra; 5km, exit 11 Telhal; r'bout, left to Sabugo, 2nd right after Ó Lisboa restaurant, 50m, left.

Duarte D'Eça Leal
Rua Nossa Senhora da Piedade 25,
Sabugo, Almargem do Bispo,
2715-452 Sintra

Tel	+351 219 624354
Email	duarte@shepinetree.com
Web	www.shepinetree.com

Quinta do Scoto

The manor house was built in 1746 for the chaplain of the Marques de Pombal and much of his magnificent furniture remains. This has been an epic restoration for English owners Penny and Tony who have fascinating stories to tell; note the tiled friezes inside and the stone aqueducts in the grounds. Your hosts couldn't be nicer or more helpful, they're child-friendly, have a daughter of their own, Charlotte, and have thought of everything to make your stay special. Big, elegant bedrooms — two in the house, the rest in the barn — are uncluttered and TV-free; bathrooms are spotless and new; one bath has been made from a wine press. Being so close to Lisbon — on the seam of suburbia and the rural beyond — there's lots to see and do: Sintra, Obidos, beaches, all a train ride away. Breakfasts set you up beautifully for a busy day (homemade scones, chutneys, jams, eggs from their hens), the saltwater pool, lined with striped loungers, is a dream to come home to; there are ponies to ride and Izzy — the Portuguese waterdog — is the star of the show. Space and comfort in great measure… and perfect peace under the stars.

Price	€65–€130.
Rooms	8 suites for up to 6.
Meals	Restaurants & cafés 5 to 10-minute walk.
Closed	Never.
Directions	A16, exit 12 for Meleças, right at r'bout. At next r'bout, 2nd exit. Next r'bout, 1st exit 'Transito Local', right at T-junc., then left; left again, over stone bridge, Quinta on right.

Tony Ross
Rua Dr. Teixeira Bastos, Melecas,
2635-314 Sintra

Mobile	+351 913 037521
Email	tonyandpenny@quintadoscoto.com
Web	www.quintadoscoto.com

Pensão Residencial Sintra

Many love the faded grandeur that envelops this family-run B&B, built on a thickly wooded hillside as a viscount's summer retreat in the days when Sintra was a hill station to the gentry. It became a B&B in 1958. An original bannistered staircase winds up to enormous bedrooms with high ceilings, wooden floors and somewhat old-fashioned furniture and fittings; there's a distinctly out-of-time feel but ask for one with a mountain view — they're spectacular. The more modern rooms are quite functional in style. Downstairs is an enormous dining room where snacks are available until 11pm; if the weather's good, tuck into afternoon tea on the expansive terrace with beguiling views to the Moorish castle. Or doze in a deckchair in the delightful garden that drips with greenery; enjoy the lovely old trees (plane, lemon, palm, magnolia), the swimming pool below, and the small play area for children. Down the road is Bica de São Pedro, a friendly restaurant where the owner herself works. Numerous shops are a short stroll; steeply atmospheric paths wind up to Sintra's magical castles and palaces.

Price	€50–€90. Singles €45–€85.
Rooms	15: 7 twin/doubles, 8 doubles. Extra beds available.
Meals	Snacks available all day, from €3. Packed lunches. Restaurant 500m.
Closed	Rarely.
Directions	From Lisbon, IC19 exit for Sintra & São Pedro. Follow São Pedro & Centro Histórico. Hotel signed on right as you exit São Pedro, towards historic centre of Sintra.

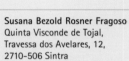

Susana Bezold Rosner Fragoso
Quinta Visconde de Tojal,
Travessa dos Avelares, 12,
2710-506 Sintra

Tel	+351 219 230738
Email	pensao.residencial.sintra@clix.pt
Web	www.residencialsintra.blogspot.com

Casa Miradouro

In a tranquil 'suburb' of old Sintra, steeply down the hill from the centre, is wonderful 'Douro View House', named for its end-of-road views. Gaze up at the Moorish Castle or down to glorious green hills. Outside and inside this 1890s summer house you get a marvellous sense of light and space: when the sun shines, rooms and corridors are awash with light. New Belgian owners, father Luc and daughter Charlotte, have painted the lovely plasterwork white and exposed the fine oak floors; the house shines. They meet, greet and help every guest that comes, are knowledgeable about Portuguese food and wine and welcome all ages. All is immaculate but nothing feels precious. There are three charming sitting rooms with newspapers, drinks, sweeties and nespresso on tap; chess boards and magazines, too. Light, airy, uncluttered bedrooms, some with coir carpets, some with stucco ceilings, all with beds wrapped in delicious linen, have private balconies or a piece of terrace; double glazing and heating make them super cosy in winter. Birds trill; breakfasts on the terrace are a joy. And Lisbon is a train trip away.

Price	€95–€135. Single €85–€120. Triple €115–€155.
Rooms	8: 4 doubles, 2 twins/doubles, 1 triple, 1 single.
Meals	Packed lunch €7. Restaurant 500m.
Closed	Mid to end-January.
Directions	From Lisbon, IC19 to Sintra. Signs for Centro Histórico. At square by palace, right (in front of Hotel Central) & on to Tivoli Hotel. Down for 400m. House on left.

Charlotte Lambregts
Rua Sotto Mayor 55,
2710-801 Sintra

Tel	+351 219 107100
Email	mail@casa-miradouro.com
Web	www.casa-miradouro.com

Quinta Verde Sintra

Nature surrounds you: this modern house, midway between Sintra and the beaches, set well back from the road, is wrapped around by honeysuckle, palms, bay trees, cedar, succulents, and green hills beyond. It's a warm, family-run B&B thanks to Cesaltina, her husband, sons, grandchildren and three dogs; there's a lovely, easy, friendly feel. Bedrooms display a mix of wooden and metal beds, a few antiques, pretty lights, Arroiolos tapestries, embroidered curtains, crisp linen and small rugs on tiled floors. Bathrooms sparkle. You breakfast on bread baked in a wood-fired oven and homemade jam, in the conservatory or out on the terrace, overlooking a pool with views of the lush Sintra hills; on a clear day you should see the Castle of the Moors, Pena Palace, Monserrate House, the Quinta da Regaleira and the Palácio de Seteais. As for the two self-catering apartments, they're set apart from the main house and have good-sized sitting rooms and well-equipped kitchens; one has an open fire, the other a sitting area under a shower of pink roses. Excellent fish restaurants are a short drive.

Price	€70–€100. Singles €60–€90. Apts €100–€150 per night.
Rooms	4 + 2: 3 doubles, 1 suite for 4. 2 apts for 4.
Meals	Light lunch available. Dinner, 3 courses, €17. Wine €10. By arrangement.
Closed	Rarely.
Directions	From Sintra, down to Ribeira de Sintra, then Várzea de Sintra. After 1km, right at x-roads signed Magoito. Uphill for 1.5km, on right.

Cesaltina de Sena
Estrada de Magoito 84,
Casal da Granja/Varzea de Sintra,
2710-252 Sintra

Tel	+351 219 616069
Email	mail@quintaverdesintra.com
Web	www.quintaverdesintra.com

Convento de São Saturnino

Deep in Azóia's valley something magical has happened. On the site of a ruin stand a series of buildings based on a 12th-century convent, the vision of talented owners. Whitewashed, inter-connecting spaces, curved roofs, winding steps, sparkling sea glimpses and a trickling spring – it's a place to lose yourself in. Weathered beams, sloping ceilings, ancient shutters... each bedroom has its own charm, each is cosily stylish and deeply inviting. Fabrics are rich, bathrooms are pampering. In the big communal living area are squidgy sofas, gorgeous books, a collection of scrolls and artefacts found on the site. Nod hello to dogs, donkeys, geese and hens, take a dip in the saltwater pool, scramble down to the sea, or lounge on a rock and breathe it all in: the pine, the eucalyptus and the sea. (Add to this a shiatsu massage and your bliss will be complete.) There are three great restaurants within walking distance, one housed in an old windmill. The atmosphere in this small hotel is homely, the views are restorative and one of the best beaches in all Portugal is a 30-minute walk. Enchanting.

Price	€130-€200. Singles from €120.
Rooms	9: 3 doubles, 3 twins, 3 suites.
Meals	Occasional lunch, snacks & dinner. Restaurants walking distance.
Closed	Never.
Directions	A5 Lisboa-Cascaís, exit Malveira/Aldeia do Junto. 4km after Malveira da Serra, left for Cabo da Roca. At Moinho D. Quixote bear right; signed.

John Nelson Perrie
Azóia, Cabo da Roca,
2705-001 Sintra

Tel	+351 219 283192
Email	contact@saosat.com
Web	www.saosat.com

As Janelas Verdes

In the old city, just yards from the Museum of Ancient Art, is an aristocratic townhouse, 19th-century home of the novelist Eça de Queirós. It's the perfect place to lay your head when in Lisbon and from the moment you are greeted by smiling Palmira you feel like an honoured guest. To one side of the reception are a handsome fireplace, a piano and comfortable chairs, and marble-topped tables for breakfast in winter. Summer breakfasts – and candlelit aperitifs – are enjoyed on a cobbled patio where a fountain gurgles and bougainvillea runs riot. Inside, a grand old spiral staircase lined with Bordalo Pinheiro cartoons takes you up to bedrooms comfortable and quietly charming. Expect Portuguese repro beds, smart curtains, pale carpets, pastel colours, dressing gowns and towels embroidered with the JV logo. (And instead of a 'do not disturb' sign there's a hand-embroidered pillow that says 'shhh!'). Some rooms have impressive views of the river Tejo – book early if you want one. A delectable small hotel, enlarged to include a cosy library on the top floor with an honesty bar and a lovely convivial feel.

Price	€157-€298. Singles €143-€280.
Rooms	29 twins/doubles.
Meals	Breakfast €14. Restaurants nearby.
Closed	Never.
Directions	A2 over river Tejo, exit for Alcântara. Over r'bout; follow tram route for 500m. Hotel on right, close to Museu de Arte Antiga. Cais Rocha tramline five-minute walk.

The Cardoso & Fernandes Families
Rua das Janelas Verdes 47,
1200-690 Lisbon

Tel	+351 213 968143
Email	janelas.verdes@heritage.pt
Web	www.heritage.pt

Chiado 16

Tucked into a hill that swoops from upscale Chiado to busy Baixa in Lisbon's heart, a chic ensemble of apartments for couples and families. From the chandelier'd reception's mosaic floor to the Nespresso machine and super-speed internet, everything in this historic townhouse – restored by an award-winning architect – is modern and top quality. The one at the top has the best views of castle and river, but all are lovely: bright, contemporary, intimate, each with a fully equipped kitchen, laundry, heaps of storage space and insulation to mute the city buzz. Large mirrors reflect the bright sofas and stylish coffee tables that pose on gleaming wood floors in the sitting room, and TVs are sunk into white walls. Soak in a large marble tub, doze off under satin sheets; there's room service, a daily maid, and a generous light breakfast arrives each morning. Heleen (Dutch, New Zealand-raised, in Lisbon for 22 years) lives above with her family and will help with tours, fado evenings, gym, babysitting, massage, parking space… and the best restaurants in fun Bairro Alto up the hill. A stunning city-centre space.

Price	€200-€250.
Rooms	4 apartments for 2-4.
Meals	Breakfast included. Partner restaurant next door. Lunch €23. Dinner €35.
Closed	Never.
Directions	From metro Baixa Chiado, down Rua Garrett; 3rd street on right to Largo da Academia square at end, Chiado 16 on left side of square.

Heleen Rosa da Silva
Largo da Academia das Belas Artes 16,
1200-005 Lisbon

Tel	+351 213 941616
Email	info@chiado16.com
Web	www.chiado16.com

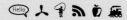

Hotel Britânia

One street back from Av. da Liberdade, this gem of a hotel was designed by Cassiano Branco and ranks among Lisbon's classified buildings. Art Deco meets ocean liner: it's a museum piece. The fun begins in the reception area which sports twin ranks of marble columns, black and grey striped chairs, port-holed doors and a huge globe; renovation revealed Adamastor, the sea monster from Camoes' *Lusiades*, and the showpiece, a retro barber's shop. A wood and chrome staircase leads to the bedrooms (there's a lift too); all enormous, with private entrance halls, decked terraces on the top floor, original cork parquet floors, funky steel tubular lamps and original Estremoz-marble bathrooms with deep sinks and tubs. You are offered sparkling Portuguese wine at breakfast, served impeccably in your room – or in a bar adorned with period photos of the feminist legend Natália Correia, who once lived here. There are paperbacks aplenty to swap in the book-exchange library, and the Glória funicular to ferry you to cool Bairro Alto. No view but wonderful staff and masses of charm.

Price	€143–€255. Singles €130–€230. Suite €475.
Rooms	33: 32 twins/doubles, 1 suite.
Meals	Breakfast €14. Restaurants nearby.
Closed	Never.
Directions	Signs to centre & Pr. Marquês de Pombal, then towards Pr. dos Restauradores. Left before Metro 'Avenida'. Rodrigues Sampaio one street east of Av. da Liberdade, on right.

The Alves Sousa & Fernandes Families
Rua Rodrigues Sampaio 17,
1150-278 Lisbon

Tel	+351 213 155016
Email	britania.hotel@heritage.pt
Web	www.heritage.pt

Casa Villa Serra & Casa Pátria

A brilliant opportunity to live as a Lisboeta. Up a dozen cobbled alleys – or the funicular should the steps prove exhausting – to arrive at these neighbouring houses, perched high above the city centre. Casa Pátria is a three-storey house for four: contemporary, open-plan, with a clever, funky use of space and filled with light from top to toe. Find a cream sofa, an antique bed, a well-equipped kitchen beneath a sky light, and a lovely open-tread staircase up to a living room and a split-level roof terrace: what views! Villa Serra too is full of views, and has three double bedrooms, the smallest making up for its size with a throne-like Bilros bed. Find marble, granite and cork floors, smart brown leather sofas, a 180-degree panorama from the living room, and more views from the garden terrace – sit out here with a nice cold glass of vinho verde and a fresh slab of cod roasting on the barbecue. Portugal's queen of fado, Amalia Rodrigues, was born just around the corner and now her nephew offers exclusive fado tours to guests. *Minimum three nights. Ask about volunteering & cookery classes.*

Price	House €240-€350. House €180-€250. Prices per night.
Rooms	House for 2-6. House for 1-4.
Meals	Restaurants within walking distance.
Closed	Never.
Directions	Above Praça dos Restauradores in Lisbon's old town. Detailed directions on booking.

Debra Kleber
Rua Joaquina 5,
1150-197 Lisbon

Mobile	+351 913 464517
Email	deb@VisitingPortugal.com
Web	www.visitingportugal.com/casavillaserra.htm

Casa Santana & Casa Travessa

Down a cobbled alley on a steepish hill are Santana and Travessa. From Santana's first-floor living room a magical view sweeps across tiled rooftops and shining river to the famous Rossio Square; from tiny ground-floor Travessa you can glimpse the majestic Igreja do Carmo, ruined in the earthquake of 1755. In Santana, a great little kitchen with chunky bar stools and an up-in-the-attic feel; in Travessa, a cool white bedroom with a carved Bilros bed and neat little kitchen. Bed linen and towels are immaculate and all you might want is here: books, toys, DVDs, stuff for the beach, vinho verde in the fridge, a laptop with WiFi. On arrival, Debra will give you a tour of the local area and, if you're interested, will suggest volunteering opportunities with local homeless and conservation charities. And fado singer Amalia Rodrique's nephew offers tours and cookery classes: learn to make *arroz de marisco* (seafood rice) – or, if you're feeling flush, let him cook for you. Restaurants, bars, shops and history lie down the hill and the beach is a train ride away. *Minimum three nights.*

Price	Apt for 2-4, €120-€150. Apt for 2, €90-€120. Prices per night.
Rooms	Apartment for 2-4. Apartment for 2.
Meals	Restaurants within walking distance.
Closed	Never.
Directions	Above Praça dos Restauradores in Lisbon's old town. Detailed directions on booking.

Debra Kleber
Rua Joaquina 5,
1150-197 Lisbon

Mobile	+351 913 464517
Email	deb@VisitingPortugal.com
Web	www.visitingportugal.com/santana.htm

Solar de Alvega

The Marquês de Pombal built it in the 18th century; it's as imposing as ever. Glamorous Maria Luiza and her English husband bought the house in 1998, restored it to its former grandeur and introduced English and Portuguese antiques: Staffordshire figures and blue and white *faience*, grandfather clocks, Portuguese flags. Maria Luiza has restored many of the antiques herself, from letter-scales to Art Nouveau lamps; should you meet her, you'll find her delightful company. Grand bedrooms (the one at the front facing the busy through road) have polished parquet floors, tapestry rugs, tasselled silk curtains, antique washstands, beds with elaborate headboards, all put together with love. The tower room has a door to a roofed balcony, another has its original pink and black marble bathroom. Note the annexe apartments are very basic. There's a games rooms that's seen better days and, in the walled garden at the back, a patio from which you can gaze down at the stream. From here a precarious walk brings you to a waterfall that powered the old mill Maria Luiza hopes still to restore. *Note that weddings are held here.*

Price	€80–€90.
Rooms	6 + 4: 6 twins/doubles. 4 apartments.
Meals	Lunch €20. Dinner €25. Wine €10–€15. By arrangement.
Closed	January to February.
Directions	From A1 Lisbon-Porto, exit Torres Novas; east on A23; exit Mouriscas. Signs for Castelo Branco & Portalegre. House 5km after exit from A23.

Luiza Mallett
EN 118-km149, Alvega,
2205-104 Abrantes

Tel	+351 241 822913
Mobile	+351 917 610579
Email	solaralvega@yahoo.co.uk
Web	www.solardealvega.com

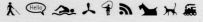

Alentejo

Monte Moita Raza & Montinho Cottage

At the end of the long winding track: two wonderful old farmhouses side by side, recently renovated and all hunky-dory, sharing a pool and gorgeous green views. From the back, the eye sweeps over fields to Marvão on its craggy hill; so ancient, so special, it's a contender for World Heritage status. Such is the setting. Peter and Rosemary, attentive and charming and living nearby, recommend visits to sites, restaurants and markets (don't miss Monday's in Valencia de Alcantara) and will take you on forays in the São Mamede Natural Park, a magical area for botanists, birdwatchers and walkers; Peter has a deep local knowledge. Interiors are tastefully contemporary, ample yet cosy, not fancy or frilly, with well-stocked kitchens, lovely modern bathrooms, superb beds, and blissfully TV-free. WiFi, wood-burners, games, toys, music and DVDs ensure cosy evenings in, there are terraces for sitting out under the stars and heaps of generous extras: mountain bikes, two donkeys and a mule to ride, wine and bread on arrival, and the use of the farm's organic oil during your stay. *Houses available separately or together.*

Price	House €760-€1,100. Cottage €550-€860. Prices per week.
Rooms	House for 4-9. Cottage for 2-4.
Meals	Restaurant 5km.
Closed	Never.
Directions	From Lisbon, A1 dir. Porto; exit 7 onto A23; exit 15 onto IP2 south, dir. Portalegre. Left at Alpalhão, right in town for Castelo de Vide, then Marvão.

Peter & Rosemary Eden
Vale de Rodam,
7330-151 Marvão

Tel	+351 962 467875
Mobile	+351 962 467875
Email	peter_eden@hotmail.com
Web	www.wildportugal.com

Quinta da Dourada

Irrepressible Nuno has left careers in bullfighting and publishing to restore his heritage: a pretty farm in a lush setting. The main farmhouse and much of the land has been lost over the years but from the remaining buildings your charming host has created an authentic and comfortable place to stay. The low-pitched family 'chalet', the nucleus of Dourada, is linked to the largest apartment by means of a terrace with a soaring roof, a semi open-air area where you may linger over drinks and stargaze at an unpolluted sky. The apartments are single-storey and rustic in style, with dark beams criss-crossing ceilings and simple rugs softening black slate floors. Walls are white, spotlights sparkle, sofas have throws. There are smart white showers, teensy kitchenettes and white linen bread bags to hang outside your door for the morning delivery. So much to enjoy here: hammocks strung in strategic places and bikes to borrow, basketball, mini football, ping-pong, even tastings of the Quinta's wine. Pathways edged with dry-stone walls lead to the remains of an old sweet-chestnut plantation and a blissful big pool.

Price	€85. Apartments €595 per week.
Rooms	2 + 4: 2 doubles. 3 apartments for 2, 1 apartment for 4.
Meals	Breakfast included. Local meals delivered. Restaurant 10-min drive.
Closed	Never.
Directions	From Portalegre, follow Serra & Solão Frio. After Solão Frio, Quinta signed on left 2km after x-roads to S. Bento; continue 900m over bridge to house.

Nuno Malato Correia
Serra de S. Mamede,
Ribeira de Niza,
7300-409 Portalegre

Mobile	+351 937 218654
Email	quintadadourada@iol.pt
Web	www.quintadadourada.com

Quinta Vale de Marmélos

Gaze on Spain from your bedroom window, across butterfly-sprinkled citrus and olive groves. The two-hectare gardens grow everything from figs to kumquats; the farm became a nursery almost by default when people kept asking for cuttings. Brush against lavender and other fragrant bushes on the drive up to this neo-gothic building with extraordinarily high ceilings. Friendly, dedicated and impressively integrated in local life, Tim and Ann strike a beautiful balance between being welcoming and leaving you to your own devices. Bedrooms are not fancy but simple, spotless and furnished with Alentejan hand-painted furniture; we'd choose the one with the veranda. Tim offers a guided tour to the lesser known parts of the fascinating walled town of Elvas on the Spanish border, famous for its crystallised plums (Lord Wellington exported them to Fortnum & Mason). In the rambling, shady grounds are chickens, whose eggs often make the breakfast table, snoozing cats and a pair of resident owls. The quinta is interesting for gardeners and birdwatchers and pretty good value, too.

Price	€55–€75. Cottages €375 per week.
Rooms	4 + 2: 2 doubles, 1 twin; 1 twin with separate shower. 2 cottages for 2-4.
Meals	Restaurants 3km. Dinner for late arrivals.
Closed	Rarely.
Directions	Lisbon A6 dir. Spain, exit for Elvas. To aqueduct; over 2 r'bouts, right for Olivenca at 3rd with fireman statue; on for 3km, till flags.

Tim & Ann Claye
7350-111 Elvas

Tel	+351 268 626193
Mobile	+351 963 726237
Email	annietimbo@yahoo.com
Web	www.quintavaledemarmelos.co.uk

Casa do Terreiro do Poço

Once upon a time this long dazzling white house was home to six families. There were just two old ladies left when João and Rita bought it; two rooms are named in their honour. João is a lawyer but passionately interested in décor (he has an antique shop, too); Rita is an interior designer. Perfectionists, they have remodelled the house and transformed it into a fascinating, even exotic B&B. Outbreaks of flamboyance – silk curtains, ornate bedheads, ragged walls, cut-glass mirrors – are saved from being 'over the top' by the occasional intervention of rough, natural stone, a simple colourwashed wall, crisp unadorned linen... The house is in the centre of Borba, so views (apart from in the tower suite) are over the small public garden at the front or the garden and pool at the back. Overlooking the pool is a long pavilion and a delightful area for guests to sit, while enormous terracotta pots are dotted about and scattered trees provide plenty of shade. Breakfast is fresh and varied and the local restaurants are good; ask João about the wonderful adega nearby. *Min. two nights in summer & at weekends.*

Price	€75–€170.
Rooms	8: 1 double, 1 twin/double, 5 suites for 2, 1 suite for 4.
Meals	Lunch & dinner with wine, €35. By arrangement.
Closed	Rarely.
Directions	From A6, exit 8 to N4 & Borba. Follow Rua de S. Bartholomeu, house on left after church (behind public garden).

Rita & João Cavaleiro Ferreira
Largo dos Combatentes da
Grande Guerra 12, 7150-152 Borba

Mobile	+351 917 256077
Email	geral@casadoterreirodopoco.com
Web	www.casadoterreirodopoco.com

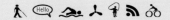

Herdade de Maroteira

Tradition and family run deep in rural Alentejo, and nowhere more so than at this cork farm in the hills. Philip and Margarida are the fifth generation to strip their oaks by hand each June, keep chickens, sheep, cows, and let black pigs loose on the acorns (they give 'porco preto' its sweet taste). Oh, and Philip makes award-winning wine. What a pleasure to buy the farm's fresh fruit, honey, lamb, eggs, then take a picnic to the estate's highest point, where views swoop over forest and plains. The handsome farmhouse, white with a splash of sunny yellow, is home to the couple and their two boys, with one half handed over to guests. It's grand without pretensions: hats hung in the entrance hall, an antiquey sitting room with a vaulted ceiling and black-and-white tiles, a large kitchen, a terrace with a swing. If rustic and cosy is your thing, pick the shepherd's cottage next door for its sunny beamed sitting room and palm-shaded terrace. Borrow the dogs for walks, stroll to the atmospheric spring-fed pool, discover fine craftsmanship in the 'marble towns', bask in the family's old-fashioned friendliness. A gem.

Price	Farmhouse wing €450-€575. Cottage €380-€450. Prices per week.
Rooms	Farmhouse wing for 2-5. Cottage for 2-5.
Meals	Dinner with wine, €25. By arrangement.
Closed	Never.
Directions	From Evora N254 to Redondo, then N381 for Estremoz. As road climbs to Aldeia da Serra, winery on left. Soon after, left signed Maroteira.

Philip Mollet
Aldeia da Serra, Aldeia da Serra,
7170-120 Redondo

Tel	+351 266 909823
Mobile	+351 966 548697
Email	philipmollet@gmail.com
Web	www.maroteira.com

Quinta da Espada

Quinta da Espada: Quinta of the Sword. The sword in question was hidden on this farm by Geraldo Geraldes, who snatched Évora back from the Moors. With views down to this lovely city, surrounded by cork oaks and olive groves, is a peaceful, mimosa-graced farmhouse. Simply furnished bedrooms with delicately hand-painted Alentejan beds vary in size and colour; terracotta tiles, *estera* matting and dark beams create a country mood; bathrooms are spotless. The Green Room occupies what was once the tiny family chapel, and the smaller sitting room, where you breakfast before a lit hearth in winter, is particularly charming, its shelves crammed with Alentejan artefacts. Independence lovers will be happy here; most rooms are separate from the owner's house and breakfast is left for you in the guest kitchen; rustle up your own meal and take it to a smartly cobbled terrace. You can leave the car behind and follow the tracks that lead to Évora from the estate – or follow the trail along the aqueduct, then return to ping-pong and pool. Bliss in summer. *Minimum stay three nights in apartments.*

Price	€89. Singles €58. Suite €107. Apartments €190 (€1,140 per week).
Rooms	5 + 2: 4 doubles, 1 suite. 2 apartments for 4-5.
Meals	Breakfast for self-caterers €9. Lunch & dinner €30, by arrangement. Wine €10.
Closed	24-25 December.
Directions	From Évora towards Arraiolos. After 4km, Quinta signed to right.

Maria Isabel Sousa Cabral
Apartado 68, Estrada de Arraiolos km4,
7002-501 Évora

Tel	+351 266 734549
Email	isabelcabral@quintadaespada.com
Web	www.quintadaespada.com

Entry 54   Map 4

Herdade do Passareiro

Passareiro has been in an Anglo-Portuguese family for five generations: rustic Alentejo meets English eccentricity. The owners of this lovely old Alentejo farmhouse greet you on arrival in a cobbled courtyard dotted with loquat trees, and a housekeeping couple live next door. Inside feels like the family home it still is. Landed-gentry interiors exude an understated charm, furnishings are traditional but not over-styled, hats and green wellies line up by the door and there are books, giant fireplaces and a tiled mural of two much-loved former employees in the great country kitchen. Black pigs snuffle acorns in winter, source of the delicious 'porco preto' you find in your welcome hamper, along with olives and bread. The large rose-fringed terrace at the back is delicious for relaxing but the pièce de résistance is the pool: a glorious folly overlooking vineyards, fed by a natural spring. Sit back and watch the rays of the sun soften on immaculate white and Alentejo-yellow walls. White viognier is grown here; walks guide you through vineyards, ancient cork forests and olive groves. Heaven. *Chef available.*

Price	€400-€450 per night (€1,950-€2,950 per week).
Rooms	House for 10-12.
Meals	Restaurant 2km.
Closed	Never.
Directions	A2 from Lisbon; then A6. Exit junc. 5 dir. Montemor, then N370 to S. Sebastiao (10 mins). Signed entrance 2 mins outside S.Sebastiao, on right, before big cedars.

Joana Mollet
Nossa Senhora da Boa Fe,
7000-013 Évora

Tel	+44 (0)20 7351 1769
Mobile	+44 (0)7930 993183
Email	stay@passareiro.com
Web	www.passareiro.com

Monte Saraz

In an unsung region of Portugal, set among ancient olive trees below medieval Monsaraz, is a serene cluster of whitewashed farm and mill buildings; Monte Saraz is utterly beautiful. Step inside. Dutch Marc, with a background in sustainable development, has put his rustic-minimalist stamp on 18th-century vaulted brick ceilings, flagstone floors and wooden doors, and made the place his own. Rooms glow with Indian kilim rugs, fine country furniture, beautiful examples of arts and crafts and washes of warm colour. All is cool and calm. There's a communal sitting room filled with flowers, three charming suites in Alentejan style, stylish all-white bathrooms, and four delightful self-catering 'cottages', all with outdoor spaces. Outside are lovely orchards, gardens and peaceful shady corners, and two pools, one framed by the arches of the original olive press – exquisite. Marc and Luz Maria, easy-going, open-hearted and friendly, serve you delicious breakfasts Portuguese style, and the views of Monsaraz, perched on its hilltop, are stunning – particularly poignant when floodlit at night. Great value.

Price	Suite €75. Cottage €100 (€665 per week).
Rooms	3 + 4: 3 suites. 4 cottages for 2-4.
Meals	Restaurants nearby.
Closed	January.
Directions	From Évora, N258 to Reguengos de Monsaraz, São Pedro de Corval & Monsaraz. 6km after São Pedro, left signed Monte Saraz, Oliva de Pega; thro' olive grove; at T-junc., right, then straight; 1st group of houses.

Marc P. Lammerink
Horta dos Révoredos, Barrada,
7200-172 Monsaraz

Tel	+351 266 557385
Email	info@montesaraz.com
Web	www.montesaraz.com

Cortinhas

You arrive at the back... to what seems like a tiny house limewashed in ochre. Inside, a surprising sense of space, more than enough for four; outside, a lush garden and a veranda with views to the coast on a clear day. All is airy and sunny, artistic and homely, with soothing colours and unglazed terracotta floors. The lofty, white-raftered living space is rustic and charming, with sofa and sofabed, wood-burner, pictures and books; the kitchen is lovely. The powder-blue bedroom opens to a corner of the terrace, the twin room is white and cool. The owners live next door; Sophie's green fingers have nurtured the wisteria and plumbago that romps all over the house, and the herbs and flowers that peep through every window. There's a sweet old horse in the olive orchard, the garden leads to a meadow – a picture in spring – and there's a small lake minutes away, good for swimming in early summer; sheep bells tinkle in the distance. Behind, on the edge of hills, are eucalyptus, olives and oaks, good walks (let Tuke guide you) and masses of birdlife. Pretty beaches are 12km away, and wild surfing beaches not much further.

Price	€60-€72 (€490-€590 per week).
Rooms	House for 4-6 (1 double, 1 twin; sofabed). Extra bed available.
Meals	Restaurants 3km.
Closed	Rarely.
Directions	From Cercal, south for Odemira. After S. Luis, right at cemetery for Val Bejinha; 2km on, right at mail boxes, left at top.

Sophie & Tuke Taylor
Vale Bejinha, 2581 Cx. S. Luis,
7630-489 Odemira

Tel +351 283 976076
Email walkdontwalk80@hotmail.com

Monte Maravilhas

Get to know the real Portugal: Prem organises hiking and biking weeks (yoga, painting, Portuguese and meditation/massage courses, too) and provides proper walking maps. It's believed that the abundance of water here, in this otherwise thirsty region, is the reason why Monte 'Miracles' is so named: there are no fewer than four wells within the 22-acre estate and their water is sweet and drinkable. At the top of a long hillside track, the grounds are quite lovely, furnished with figs, vines and olive trees; the farmer next door turns the olives into oil, the grapes into wine and dries the figs for winter. Such is the setting for these houses (two of which interconnect), the largest being the old farmhouse, simply and stylishly converted by Prem. The beams, stones and wooden floors are as they were; new pale pine, huge stoves and white walls add to the rustic feel. There's a lovely saltwater pool to come home to, a hammock between the orange trees, and Prem on hand to give massages for aching bones. Meals are not provided but your serene hostess will cook by arrangement for groups. Simply lovely. *Min. stay one week.*

Price	€390-€680 per week.
Rooms	3 houses: 2 for 4, 1 for 6.
Meals	Restaurants 1km.
Closed	Never.
Directions	From Faro A2 to Lisboa; exit 13, Santana da Serra. Follow São Martinho das Amoreiras, 1km before town, left signed 'Maravilhas'. Follow dirt track for 500m.

Prem Zijtveld
São Martinho das Amoreiras,
7630-527 Odemira

Tel	+351 283 925397
Mobile	+351 964 235864
Email	info@montemaravilhas.com
Web	www.montemaravilhas.com

Entry 58   Map 5

Herdade do Touril

Hear the waves crashing on windy days – you're as near to the coast as you can get without falling into the sea! Owner Luis, who lives in Lisbon, has taken over the big family estate and added a luxurious spin; more hotel than *herdade*, Touril is an impeccable place to stay. Surrounded by sunflowers (perfect symbol of the Alentejo), fields of cattle and well-manicured lawns, the reconstructed house and its farm buildings ooze contemporary style and natural good taste. Bougainvillea romps on terraces, guests meet over barbecues and sleek pool, and farm implements are artfully displayed in reception, along with hay bales and wooden sheep – a picturesque homage to rusticity. B&B rooms and self-catering studios spread themselves over the main house and whitewashed outbuildings, all a decent distance apart. You may not get Algarvian temperatures but, within the protected Parque Natural, this is bliss for those who seek tranquillity: walk across the cliffs to secluded beaches, seek out rare nesting storks, spin off on a bike to Zambujeira for cool bars and surfers – and a music festival in August.

Price	€80–€140. Houses €150–€280. Apts €130–€220. Prices per night.
Rooms	12 + 5: 12 twins/doubles. 2 houses for 5; 3 apts for 2.
Meals	Restaurant 2km.
Closed	Never.
Directions	In Zambujeira do Mar, follow main road round to right, keep going for 2km, then right for 2km. Herdade do Touril on left.

Luis Falcão
7630-734 Zambujeira do Mar

Tel	+351 283 950080
Mobile	+351 937 811627
Email	reservas@touril.pt
Web	www.herdadedotouril.pt

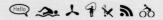

Quinta do Barranco da Estrada

Hugging the shore of one of the Alentejo's largest freshwater lakes, the Quinta is a paradise of wild beauty. The area has a microclimate so the swimming season is long, and spring's wild flowers will enchant you. Frank's eco-friendly renovation of the original low house took years and then a row of guest rooms was added. These are light, cool and pleasingly simple, with terraces and gorgeous lake views. The big extended living room and bar share one sociable space and embrace Portuguese and English styles of décor; now, thanks to the arrival of new wife Daniella and her family, there's a wonderfully warm happy feel. Beyond huge windows is a vine-festooned terrace for sultry summer days; further butterfly-bright terraces brim over with hibiscus, oleander, palm, jasmine, plumbago, cactus. Follow the path to the jetty where you can canoe, fish for crayfish, sail, sunbathe on the lawns, stroll around the lake, perhaps in the company of Frank's dogs. Delightful Frank will help with the naming of all those birds; the whole remote place is a birdwatcher's dream.

Price	€64–€165. Singles €56–€165. Family €100–€165. Extra bed €25.
Rooms	12: 10 twins/doubles, 2 family suites.
Meals	Lunch €15. Dinner €22.50. Wine from €6.50. Restaurants 13km.
Closed	Rarely.
Directions	From S. Martinho das Amoreiras, dir. Portimão. At T-junc., left to Monchique; 8km, left to Cortes Pereiras; 8.5km, right. Map on website.

Frank McClintock
7665-880 Santa Clara-a-Velha

Tel	+351 283 933065
Email	info@paradiseinportugal.com
Web	www.paradise-in-portugal.com

The Yurt

No mobile, no WiFi, no roads, no noise – just the birds to wake you and the stars to twinkle you to sleep. This lovely new yurt (with a rainproof sky light) sits in a magical valley surrounded by cork oaks, madronho, tree heather, viburnum and gorse; wild flowers burst forth in spring. Carol's renovated farmhouse lies two steep terraces above. She, artist, massage therapist, eco warrior and inspired cook, has lived in Portugal for 25 years and gives you breakfast as and when you like it (homemade bread, scones, jams, marmalade, yogurts, fruits) and dinners (rustic Mediterranean, organic home-grown veg, rich Alentejan wines) in her big farmhouse kitchen or on her wisteria'd veranda, shared with the friendly volunteers who help on her tree-planting projects. A short walk brings you to a cool lake and an elegant row boat; you can take a picnic to the island and swim. Return to Persian rugs, hammocks, fluffy bathrobes, a feather down duvet on a comfortable bed, a solar-heated shower and a proper old-fashioned wooden privy – as lavish as nature allows. For urban escapees: sheer bliss. *Minimum two nights.*

Price	€75. Extra bed €15.
Rooms	Yurt for 2-4.
Meals	Lunch €15. Dinner with wine, €20. By arrangement. Summer kitchen (no cooker). Restaurant 10km.
Closed	November to mid-April.
Directions	From S. Martinho das Amoreiras for Portimão. At T-junc., left to Monchique; 8km, left to Cortes Pereiras; after 5.5km dirt track, right at sign, down hill to house.

Carol Dymond
Alvorada, Retorta, Cortes Pereiras,
7665-859 Santa Clara-a-Velha

Tel	+351 283 933244
Mobile	+351 934 793168
Email	dymondcarol@yahoo.com
Web	www.alvorada.blog.com/room

Algarve

Casa Vicentina

This west coast deserves visitors, not developers; *turismo rural* is the answer. Rebuilt with imagination and eco awareness, the Casa is a reconstructed, much extended farmhouse, run by charming owners Fatima and José, he a retired civil servant with excellent English (and seven dogs!). It's a wonderful summer retreat, with little outdoor sitting areas shielded by whitewashed buttresses, and, alongside the waterlily'd lake, a super big pool. There's a grassed and fenced playground with swings and a slide, and heaps of bamboos and trees; the whole place sparkles inside and out. Now a new building completes the horseshoe layout, holding four superb suites: sitting/dining rooms, kitchenettes and bathrooms below, and bedrooms on the mezzanine: contemporary, fun. The older rooms have a Moroccan feel with their colourful cushions and rugs; most have French windows opening to the lawns and you can catch the distant sea over the tops of the eucalyptus. Masses to do – you can be at the beach in 15 minutes if you pedal hard enough (take the bikes) and the walking all year round is marvellous.

Price	€75–€165.
Rooms	12: 6 suites, 6 suites for 2-4 with kitchenette.
Meals	Light meals available. Restaurant 2km.
Closed	Never.
Directions	From Lisbon A2 for Algarve. Exit for Sines, Odemira & Lagos; follow signs for Lagos & Aljezur, exit just before Maria Vinagne; head towards Monte Novo.

José & Fatima Gomes de Almeida
Monte Novo, Odeceixe,
8670-312 Aljezur

Tel	+351 282 947447
Mobile	+351 917 762466
Email	geral@casavicentina.pt
Web	www.casavicentina.pt

Adega Velha & Casa Limão

An avenue of pines leads to this peaceful place in the undiscovered hills of the northern Algarve — but close enough to raid the bustling southern coast and the surfing beaches of the west. It's just the place for a family, or two. You are independent here but John and Cherry are happy to call in every so often with supplies of eggs, wine and honey if you wish. They lived here until moving to a house nearby and the rooms still bear the warmth and friendliness of their personalities; find soft lighting, wood-burning stoves, deep armchairs, bamboo ceilings, a luxurious Dutch-fitted kitchen. Linked by a long and lovely veranda, Casa Limão, the charming smaller studio, makes the place perfect for one big party. Both houses have breakfast terraces with views, over the pool or the small reservoir stocked with koi, while spread out below the old winery are its vineyards: do sample John's vintages, they are excellent. It's a deliciously quiet and private place and the magnificent pool leads to your own covered bar with hammocks — a lovely breezy spot from which to gaze across to the shimmering hills. *Minimum stay one week.*

Price	£700-£1,400 per week.
Rooms	House for 4-6. Studio for 2-4. House can be rented separately in low season.
Meals	Restaurants 5km.
Closed	Never.
Directions	5km north of São Marcos da Serra. Directions on booking.

	John Llewellyn
	Joios,
	8375-210 São Marcos da Serra
Tel	+351 283 882443
Email	johnllewellyn1@gmail.com
Web	www.algarveadega.com

Cabana dos Rouxinois

Great swathes of the Algarve coast have been consumed by developers and concrete-pourers; up in these hills, a half hour from the coast, it doesn't seem to matter. This house and cottage have some of the most exquisite views in the Algarve, the terraces are heavenly and the garden is a paradise of trees. The house is on several levels: enter at the back, step down to the living room and thence to the terrace; you will be captivated by the light, the space and the comfort. Everywhere are muted colours, good furniture, framed watercolours and gorgeous ceramics. Bedrooms, too, are lovely; one has soft blue toile de Jouy, blue and white furniture and a matching bathroom that opens to the main terrace, another a pretty pink and white theme, a private entrance and painted Alentejan furniture and bed. Housekeepers Marcía and Días are there to look after you well – you buy the food, they do the cooking. They also do the laundry, the cleaning and check the (heated) pool – and can babysit! Lavish yet elegant, Cabana dos Rouxinois belongs to an 'old' English family and little expense has been spared. *Minimum stay two nights.*

Price	£145-£430 per night.
Rooms	House for 8-10. Cottage for 5.
Meals	Housekeeper cooks. Restaurants nearby.
Closed	Rarely.
Directions	From Faro A22 for Portimão, exit 5 to Monchique; in centre, follow Foia. Left opp. 'A Rampa' restaurant & down to house.

Claire Farren
Apartado 33,
8550-255 Monchique

Tel	+44 (0)1952 238104
Mobile	+44 (0)7841 284118
Email	claire.farren@nexusinds.com
Web	www.cabanadosrouxinois.com

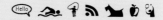

Quinta das Nascentes Altas

The view is phenomenal, sweeping down to the glittering coast. This attractive villa is built into the hillside high above the Algarve – at the top of the Foia yet below the tree line so the vegetation is lush. More than lush, thanks to numerous springs: olives, oaks, cork trees, pine, chestnut and eucalyptus burst and spill from every corner. You have three bedrooms in the main house, a double in the apartment above the garage, and a twin in the 'cottage', a hideaway for two. Every room opens onto a terrace – how could it not, with that view – while the pergola-shaded main terrace feeds off the sitting room, furnished with a glass table and fancy white chairs. There are loungers on the lawn, and a lovely large pool topped off by turquoise parasols on the next terrace up. All is hunky-dory inside and neat as a new pin: tiled floors, new rattan, striped cushions, smart kitchens – one big, one small. A sweet retreat for a Portuguese summer, but still an easy hop from surfers' paradise Arrifana or the beaches and golf courses of the Algarve. Bars, restaurants, cobbled streets? Monchique is on the windy road down.

Price	€1,050–€2,550 per week.
Rooms	House for 6–10.
Meals	Restaurants 1km.
Closed	Never.
Directions	Directions on booking.

Jean Ferran
Foia,
8550-909 Monchique

Tel	+351 282 912152
Email	ferran@monchique.com
Web	www.monchique.com

Monte Velho Nature Resort

Near to one of best beaches in Portugal, an eco resort in a gorgeous position – the rolling breakers can be seen from the house. Henrique, his partner and their young family are warm and lovely and know all the best surfing spots. Splashes of orange, blue, violet, ochre and red – not forgetting some hand-painted fish – fill this simple, stylish place with good humour. Polished floors, Indian beds, floaty fabrics, bold art, music, books and magazines add to the sense of ease; a Moroccan mood hangs in the air. Suites face south and have their own private terraces, hammocks, lanterns and rattan chairs; some get mezzanines, others wood-burning stoves, all have sitting rooms and four are brand new. Big windows pull in the view and the peace is total, in this empty, bird-rich natural park. Come evening, the west coast sunsets are inspiring, the stars dazzling. Trot off to the beach by donkey, book in a surfing lesson or a boat trip, there's 'holistic riding', too. Come home for massage, yoga, tai chi in the stunning new studio. Paradise for all seekers of harmony – and surfers, of course. *Min. seven nights July / August.*

Price	€100–€120. Suite €120–€160. Extra bed €25.
Rooms	12 doubles/suites.
Meals	Kitchen on request. Restaurants nearby.
Closed	Rarely.
Directions	From Lagos, N125 to Vila do Bispo; N268 for Aljezur & Sines. Right at sign to Vilarinha; after 800m, left to Monte Velho.

Henrique Balsemão
Bordeira,
8670-230 Carrapateira

Tel	+351 282 973207
Mobile	+351 966 007950
Email	info@montevelhoecoresort.com
Web	www.montevelhoecoresort.com

Hotel Martinhal

Come for some of the finest views in the Algarve – and to walk to Sagres peninsula, wild, wonderful and the most southwesterly point of Europe. Über-sleek on the outside, full of warmth within, the Martinhal is a modernist's dream. Each room has a wall of glass facing the sea, gliding open to lawn, balcony or decked terrace; furniture is retro Deco, materials are southern Portuguese (granite, cork, wicker, sheepskin), and lovely muted colours echo the views. The beds are lavish, the toiletries are gorgeous (Irish, organic, seaweed-based), the lighting is magical. In the restaurant, eager young staff serve scrumptious breakfasts, regional dinners with a modern twist and fish straight from the ocean; there's a chilled restaurant by one of the five pools and you can retire to cool loungers and funky beanbags. The breezes blow so you stay cool and the beach laps at your feet. If you have children, choose the resort further back from the shore, with its smart geometric houses and traditional villas, 'village square', kids' club and crèche. Back at the hotel, be lulled to sleep by the gentle swish of the sea.

Price	€139-€291. Villas & houses €139-€500.
Rooms	38: 36 doubles, 2 suites. Beach Resort: villas & houses for 4-6.
Meals	Breakfast from €5. Lunch from €10. Dinner from €15. Wine from €15.
Closed	Never.
Directions	A22 to Lagos; exit 1. At 2nd r'bout, right signed Vila do Bispo. At V. do Bispo continue on N268 to Sagres. Hotel on left, 1km before town.

Nicholas Dickinson & Nigel Chapman
Quinta do Martinhal,
8650-908 Sagres

Tel   +351 282 240200
Email   info@martinhal.com
Web   www.martinhal.com

Monte Rosa

In four hectares of unspoilt Algarve hinterland, well off the beaten track, welcoming Dutch Sandra has converted the old farmstead into a flexible, well-organised and charmingly laid back place to stay. You can go B&B or opt for the independence of self-catering: marvellous if you have children. The décor is modest but attractive, some rooms have their own kitchens, others share, and you get acres of lovely untamed space. Make friends over dinner – the dining room, open five days a week, April to November, serves tasty dishes from organic produce, with plenty for vegetarians – or around the saltwater pool. There's a free shuttle to the restaurant in the village (one mile), a daily bus to Lagos and wonderful clifftop walks on the south and west coasts; Sandra and her relaxed staff know the best spots and the surfing beaches. Massage and yoga, babysitting, riding and boat trips are bookable, there are bikes to rent, figs, plums, almonds to pluck, books and games, hammocks and hens, pathways, terraces, barbecue areas and playground... great fun, and bliss for families. *Min. four nights. Plans for sauna & jacuzzi.*

Price	€35-€65. Singles €30-€50. Family room €50-€75. House €60-€100 per night.
Rooms	7 + 3: 5 twins/doubles, 1 single, 1 family room. 3 houses for 4-8.
Meals	Breakfast €8. Dinner with wine, €18 (April-Nov). Guest kitchen.
Closed	Rarely.
Directions	From Lagos for Aljezur; after 2km through Portelas; at end of village left to Barão. House 6km on left.

Sandra Falkena
Lagoa da Rosa, 8600-016
Barão de S. João

Tel	+351 282 687002
Mobile	+351 918 552400
Email	info@monterosaportugal.com
Web	www.monterosaportugal.com

Monte da Bravura - Green Resort

Could there be a more imaginative use of old artefacts? Tables and flower beds from antique carts, an old trough for cutlery and cloths, wall partitions from recycled stone. This may be a house built from scratch, but it contains many stories — stories that your hosts are happy to share. Curious minds are encouraged and the inquisitive may stumble across a lesson in century-old traditional crop farming! This green family-run resort lies on top of a hill, framed by the sea and the mountains of Monchique. The land was inherited from Elisabete's grandfather and draws walkers to the gorgeous Barragem; don't miss the little café up at the Bravura dam. Bedrooms and apartments are clean and uncluttered, and patchwork quilts and dressers complement whitewash and terracotta. Organic, garden-fresh vegetables make an appearance at dinner, as menus tempt self-caterers away from small, perfectly formed kitchenettes. Spend the day on the beaches, return to two pools scattered with cushioned loungers, and — good news for families — a games room with billiards, table tennis and cards. *Minimum stay two nights.*

Price	€100–€160.
Rooms	6 + 6 : 6 twins/doubles. 6 apartments for 2.
Meals	Lunch €20. Dinner with wine, €30. On request.
Closed	November to March.
Directions	From Lagos, N125 to Odiáxere. Left in the centre to Barragem de Bravura, after 5km resort on the left.

Elisabete & Fernando Madeira
Cotifo,
8600-077 Bensafrim

Tel   +351 282 688175
Email   info@montedabravura.com
Web   www.montedabravura.com

Salsalito

An exotic oasis that welcoming Ralph and Sally have spent years creating – the guest book extols its virtues. It's top-drawer 'Santa Fe' – all chunky beams and tree trunk shelves. Designer Sally loves chunky jewellery and Ralph's mastery of all trades includes carpentry; his are the wardrobes, tables and lintels. Relax in the lushly tropical grounds, enjoy a pampering beauty treatment or a massage under one of the gazebos, then pad across to the pool with its tropical waterfall, overlooked by a buddha and enfolded by night-glittery trees. The honesty bar on the top terrace is a great place to meet other guests – and locals too, who pop in for a sundowner. The bedrooms are stocked with all you could want; three are in the main house and one, beside the pool with a private terrace, is delightfully Mexican in style. Nearby Burgau, with its bars and restaurants, has kept something of its old fishing village character. But you may not want to go out when there's a fabulous barbecue kitchen in the grounds for guests – you even get your own cupboard and fridge! *Min. stay three nights. Children over 13 welcome.*

Price	€55–€120 (€350–€660 per week).
Rooms	4: 3 doubles, 1 twin.
Meals	Restaurants in Burgau, 1km.
Closed	November to March.
Directions	A22 exit Lagos to Vila do Bispo onto N125. Left at lights for Almadena to end of road, then right towards Burgau. Salsalito signed on right after 1km.

	Ralph & Sally Eveleigh
	Alagoas, Estrada da Luz, Burgau,
	8600-146 Lagos
Tel	+351 282 697628
Mobile	+351 960 403748
Email	salsalitos@gmail.com
Web	www.salsalito.net

Quinta das Achadas

Hats off to owners Júlio and Jill: their Quinta is one of the most convivial of the Algarve. And the approach is a delight, through groves of olive, almond and orange trees that give way to a subtropical garden where maguey and palm, geranium and bougainvillea, pine and jasmine jostle. The living is easy here; there's a heated saltwater pool, a cabana with honesty bar, a hydromassage jacuzzi, and a grassy sports area with a small children's playground. The bedrooms, each with a small terrace, are in a converted barn and stables and overlook the gardens. Algarve-rustic, they have wooden ceilings, white walls sprinkled with art, and beautiful country antiques. Shower rooms are lovely and have Santa Katerina tiles. In colder weather you breakfast in a cosy dining room but most of the year it's mild enough to sit out on the rooftop terrace-with-views. The self-catering apartments are equally inviting; dinners, provided by Jill and Júlio, are *en famille*, delicious and generous; both used to work in the restaurant trade and combine professionalism with a warm human touch. Comfortable, relaxing, fun.

Price	€70-€120. Apartments €120-€200 per night.
Rooms	3 + 3: 3 twins/doubles. 3 apartments for 2-4.
Meals	Dinner €25-€30 (2 times a week). Wine from €7.50.
Closed	Christmas.
Directions	From Faro A22 for Vilamoura; exit 3. Straight over 1st r'bout; right for Odiaxere at 2nd. There, right at lights. Past windmill, bear left for Barragem; 1.3km on; signed.

Jill, Júlio & Isabella Pires
Estrada da Barragem, Odiáxere,
  8600-251 Lagos

Tel	+351 282 798425
Email	info@algarveholiday.net
Web	www.algarveholiday.net

Quinta Bonita Luxury Boutique Hotel

Chantelle's well-travelled parents bought this villa in 1981 as a grand holiday home. Now Chantelle and Fraser have turned it into an exceptional retreat. Chantelle does joyful front of house, Fraser is chef – and how! Terrace breakfasts flaunt pastries, fruit fresh from their own orchards and a great view of the sea; delicious lunches (on request) and tea and cakes (complimentary) are delivered to the serene outdoor pool. Bedrooms – the most peaceful at the back – are luxurious, glamorous, with hugely comfortable beds and Sky TV; contemporary bathrooms sport organic oils and rainwater showers; and there's an indoor/outdoor sitting room on whose wicker sofas you may lounge all day. The details will delight you: board games, books, exotic garden flowers… organic wines from the vineyard on the hill, bikes to borrow (Fraser is a keen cyclist) and log fires in winter. Linger on the terraces, stroll the stunning gardens, play giant chess, nip off to Lagos (castle walls, cobbled streets), discover the famous beaches. And return to this wonderful, heart-warming place. *Massage & beauty treatments available.*

Price	€95-€220.
Rooms	8 doubles.
Meals	Lunch €9-€14. Wine €7-€22. Restaurant 2km.
Closed	Rarely.
Directions	A22 to Lagos, then N125 for Sagres; after 1st traffic lights look out for entrance to parallel road (about 100m on right), follow white wall, up steep cobbled slope to Quinta.

Chantelle Kortekaas
Matos Morenos, Quatro Estradas,
8600-115 Lagos

Tel	+351 282 762135
Email	info@boutiquehotelalgarve.com
Web	www.boutiquehotelalgarve.com

Casa da Palmeirinha

It's an old house, centred on a large lush inner courtyard reminiscent of the houses of Seville; and it's bigger than it seems. José, a local journalist who speaks good English, was born here. Simple, spotless, old-fashioned bedrooms have varied views of the pretty church and village; the nicest open to a terrace and roof garden with views of the Alvor bird sanctuary, and you can cycle to it down the hill. The sitting room has flamboyant wall tiles, a gleaming terracotta floor and a rustic Spanish feel. Outside? A courtyard with an ornamental pool, and a lovely little walled swimming pool with a sun room attached; there's also a lawn shaded by arching palms. It's a cool, peaceful place to come back to, and is sometimes shared with the owner's two charming dogs. This is an unusual opportunity to stay in a Portuguese townhouse attractive both inside and out; the staff are lovely but you're left to your own devices, and you're free to make tea and coffee in the kitchen. The village is as authentic as the house and has heaps of restaurants to boot – ask José for his favourites. *Minimum two nights.*

Price	€60–€100. Singles €50–€60. Family rooms €80–€100.
Rooms	6: 2 doubles, 3 twins, 1 family suite for 2-4.
Meals	Dinner €10. Wine list or BYO. Restaurants in village.
Closed	December.
Directions	From Portimão or Lagos on N125; into Mexilhoeira Grande to church. House on left, turn left.

José Manuel Júdice Glória
Rua da Igreja 1, Mexilhoeira Grande,
8500-132 Portimão
Tel   +351 282 969277
Mobile   +351 917 546502
Email   casadapalmeirinha@gmail.com

Casa Três Palmeiras

From the Casa's perch by the cliff edge the view is a symphony of rock, sea and sky – ever-changing according to the day's mood. The villa was built in the Sixties when the Algarve was discovered, and the mood is luxurious zen... all you hear are seagulls and waves. Simple white arches and three tall palms (*três palmeiras*) soften the façade and give welcome shade once the temperatures rise. Bedrooms have everything you might expect for the price – polished floors, walk-in wardrobes, generous beds and bathrooms lavishly tiled. All feels beautifully uncluttered and four lead onto a parasoled terrace with beautiful views and a saltwater pool. It is a supremely comfortable house full of fruit and flowers, with a wood-burner for winter cosiness. The service is warm yet professional: kind Dolly, from Brazil, makes everything perfect, from massage to pedicure. A path leads from the house down to the beach; breakfast early and you may find you have it all to yourself – even in midsummer. Book ahead for high season. *Reduced green fees & car hire. Under 15s welcome for single-party bookings.*

Price	€159–€197.
Rooms	5 doubles.
Meals	Restaurants 500m.
Closed	December to January.
Directions	From Portimão, dual c'way for Praia da Rocha. Right at last r'bout for Praia do Vau; at next r'bout, double back & turn up track on right after 100m. Right along track at 1st villa.

Dolly Schlingensiepen
Apartado 84,
8501-909 Portimão
Tel   +351 282 401275
Email   dolly@casatrespalmeiras.com
Web   www.casatrespalmeiras.com

Rio Arade Manor House

Wrought-iron balustrades, colourful window mouldings and gleaming beamed ceilings – every inch the handsome Portuguese townhouse. To discover it in a former fishing village on the busy Algarve coast is a treat. This 18th-century house has been smartly modernised: step in to a cool, light space with a honey-coloured floor and creamy sofas. Behind is the dining area, traditional with rush-seated chairs and yellow china; beyond, the courtyard with its brilliant blue pool, terraces and shady corners. It's very peaceful, very Portuguese – bougainvillaea, palms, fountains and space to tuck yourself away from other guests. Sunny bedrooms are comfortable and uncluttered with breezy colour themes; some have rugs on polished wooden floors, others have creamy ceramic tiles, the best have private terraces overlooking the pool. John, affable Irishman and retired marathon runner, might join you for a barbecue with other guests. Stroll down to the river to watch the boats jostle for position, or enjoy this otherwise ordinary Algarve village come to life in July for a medieval festival.

Price	€32–€99.
Rooms	9: 3 doubles, 6 twins.
Meals	Restaurants nearby.
Closed	Rarely.
Directions	From Faro A22 for Portimao; exit 6, signs to Lagoa Sul, then Portimão. Exit for Estómbar, Ferragudo; right at r'bout to Mexilhoeira da Carregação. Large white house, wooden door 350m on left.

John O'Neill
Rua D.Joáo II 33, Mexilhoeira
de Carregação, 8400-092 Portimão

Tel	+351 282 423202
Mobile	+351 969 459029
Email	info@rioarade.com
Web	www.rioarade.com

Quinta dos Vales

Fifty hectares of vines, fruit trees, modern statuary and miniature zoo: Quinta dos Vales is magnificent. This dream kingdom of a German owner, set between the touristy west beaches and the cool surfing coast, is an unusual marriage of exotic art, goats, pigs, llamas, deer and some very fine wines – note the courtesy gift of three bottles and a basket of fresh oranges. You get several properties here, each one recently renovated, each one top-notch. The large villa, resplendent in white and terracotta, stands in its own spacious garden, up from the gleaming wine distillery and the tasting hall. The modern apartments, sharing an infinity pool, lie below; to one corner is the farm cottage. In contrast with the sun-dappled fig trees and the arcadian surroundings, pools, saunas and satellite TVs abound. A repro modernity prevails, bathrooms and kitchens are slickly contemporary and staff are kind. Stock up with provisions in the village of Estômbar, meet the locals in the restaurants and bars, and catch the coastal train; it appears to fly across the water, so close are the tracks to the sea.

Price	Manor House £1,300-£3,495. House, cottage & apts £395-£3,200. Prices per week.
Rooms	Manor house for 15. House for 8. Cottage for 4. 4 apartments for 4.
Meals	Restaurants in Estombar, 1.5km.
Closed	Never.
Directions	From Faro A22 for Portimão, exit 6; left at r'bout to Lagoa. After Lagoa, exit for Estombar. At Parchal, over railway crossing, right, then 2nd right. Signed.

Aderito Antonio
Carvoeiro Area, Parchal,
8400-031 Lagoa

Tel	+351 282 431036
Mobile	+351 914 319634
Email	enquiries@quintadosvales.eu
Web	www.quintadosvales.eu/en/home

Casa das Oliveiras

Off the beaten track, surrounded by fruit and olive trees, is this good old-fashioned B&B. It's a very friendly, very relaxing place to stay, and an affordable place from which to explore this pretty part of Portugal. You have quiet beaches 15 minutes away, and walking and cycling along the coast (and in the hills around Monchique). And Silves, with castle and cathedral, has a great choice of restaurants. Well-travelled Bill and Isa met in Angola and are charming hosts; Bill is a mine of information on local places of interest. Their modern home is spotless and traditionally furnished without fuss or frills, while spacious, comfortable bedrooms – wooden furniture, tiled floors, colourful rugs – open to the garden or the lovely big pool; one gets its own terrace. Guests come and go as they please: there are shady spots around the grounds and, for chillier days, a wood-burning stove in the sitting room. There's also a kitchen corner so you can rustle up a simple meal: excellent for families. The main road is in sight but all you hear is the rustling of the trees. Great for exploring, and brilliant value.

Price	€37–€65.
Rooms	5: 2 doubles, 3 twins. Cots & extra beds available.
Meals	Restaurants 4–6km.
Closed	Rarely.
Directions	A22 exit 7 for Alcantarilha. Leave r'bout at 1st exit towards Silves; 3km, left towards Lagoa; 4km, right just before viaduct; follow signs.

Bill & Isa Reed
Montes da Vala,
8300-044 Silves

Tel   +351 282 342115
Email   contact@casa-das-oliveiras.com
Web   www.casa-das-oliveiras.com

Quinta da Tapada do Gramacho

Down near the river, between Silves and the sea – soft hills to one side, bullrushes below – is a farmhouse that started as a mill. Imco and Karin, attentive and charming, renovated in a year and are living the dream. Dutch-restored it's as modernist as can be, full of colour and personality. Behind dazzling sleek walls lie six bedrooms, a trio of apartments and a relaxed mood: come and go as you please. There's a kitchen to rustle up a meal in, a well-stocked honesty bar, a coffee machine on tap, and each big bedroom is different – take your pick. Some open to lawn, others to terraces facing the river, all have box-spring beds with superb mattresses and robustly coloured walls – burnt orange, lime green, royal blue. But outside is where you'll mostly be, under thatch beside a cool decked pool, or enjoying breakfast in the bamboo-gravel garden; Karin bakes her own bread and makes her own jams. For dinner there's Silves, charming and historic; you can walk there. Lush beaches are a 15-minute drive, there's biking and hiking and the birdwatching's brilliant; your hosts plan to introduce hides.

Price	€65–€90. Apartments €400–795 per week.
Rooms	6 + 3: 6 doubles. 3 apartments: 2 for 2-4, 1 for 2-6.
Meals	Breakfast for self-caterers €7.50. Guest kitchen. Restaurants 1km.
Closed	Never.
Directions	A2, exit 14; N124 to Silves. Cross bridge on left; right dir. Portimão; after tunnel right at Estação, r'bout dir. Estômbar; 1km, sharp right onto track by 3 stones, 700m.

Imco & Karin
Apartado 302,
8300-999 Silves
Mobile +351 919 667048
Email info@tapadadogramacho.com
Web www.tapadadogramacho.com

The River House

Hills to climb and ride, wide open skies, and stars to take your breath away – and the occasional otter in the river. For urban escapees: a dream getaway, and a manager to hand to help you explore. Trees border one side, the land drops away on the other, the meandering river that gives the house its name becomes a lake when the dam floods (and dwindles to a stream by the end of summer). The natural garden, dotted with wildflowers, blends into the landscape. As for the lovely old terracotta-roofed house, it has undergone an exemplary, architect-designed, no-expense-spared renovation. Warm sloping timbers blend with pale walls and floors: sheer minimalist chic. White rules, with accents of colour in striped curtains and cushions, sofas are elegantly upholstered in neutral linen and the huge double-height kitchen is as stylish as they come. There are modern trestle tables, a piano to play and bold pieces of African art; a wood-burner is planned. Spin off on the bikes, go riding in the hills, stock up at the daily market in Messines, return to wicker loungers and a sweet little child-friendly infinity splash pool.

Price	£900–£2,200 per week.
Rooms	House for 6-10.
Meals	Restaurants in Messines, 3km.
Closed	Never.
Directions	Between Silves & Messines N124, turn for Amorosa follow signs for Pedreiras and continue to bridge across river, River House on right.

Cheryl Smith
8375-059 São Bartolomeu
de Messines

Tel	+44 (0)1932 244974
Mobile	+44 (0)7976 660526
Email	cheryls@vtxmarketing.co.uk
Web	www.great-locations.net

Quinta da Cebola Vermelha

So pristine one wonders how the old farmhouse can have so much personality – but it has. The owners are lovely, too: cultured, stylish, friendly, adept at combining ancient and modern yet quite capable of witty and imaginative flourishes. Much of the mood is Moroccan – but not at the hippy end of the spectrum… Bedrooms sparkle with colour, generosity and space, there are big quarry tiles and dark Indian walls with lots of paintings, some of them Noor's. The taste is refreshing, and impeccable. The roomy beds are singles side by side, the bathrooms are vast and gorgeous, and one room is in its own cottage, its shaded patio overlooking the garden. The saltwater swimming pool, too, is huge, set about with straw parasols and smart recliners, and there's a table'd lawn fragrant with orange trees to one side: bliss for a lunchtime snack. There are also some very gnarled and magnificent old olive trees. The food is the best of home cooking, the sea is 15 minutes by car, and the Algarve's hustle is safely out of reach. Let our inspector have the last word: "I defy anyone not to like it here: it is utterly gorgeous."

Price	€115–€135. Singles €95. Extra bed €30. Cot €10.
Rooms	7 doubles/twins.
Meals	Dinner, 3 courses, €29.50. Wine €15. Restaurant 1km.
Closed	Rarely.
Directions	From Faro A22 for Albufeira, exit Boliqueme. At r'bout into village; straight on, then right for Picota & Alfontes. Right; at sign to Campina, right again. Continue to house.

Ard, Noor & Bastiaan Yssel de Schepper
Campina,
8100-908 Boliqueime

Tel	+351 289 363680
Mobile	+351 938 686331
Email	info@quintadacebolavermelha.com
Web	www.quintadacebolavermelha.com

Kazuri Garden Cottages

In a lush valley a couple of miles in from the coast, long hours of sunshine and rich soil allow plants to grow in profusion. The English owner discovered this old wine farm in ruins in the early 70s and put in a fair bit of patient restoration and planting. It's a now place of peace and privacy. Behind the whitewashed outer wall the cottages stand apart from one another facing the gardens and, tucked away beyond, is an enormous round swimming pool known as 'the library'... total tranquillity. Each cottage has a terrace for sun and shade, a barbecue, a kitchen with a microwave and hob, a sitting room and double or twin bedroom with a shower: perfect for two. A mix of good art and 'jumble sale' finds, pretty dried flowers, eucalyptus beams and terracotta give a country feel, while mementos from Africa and Turkey add an exotic note. But what is most striking is the greenery: olive, pomegranate, almond and lemon trees flourish above a glistening abundance of flowers. A local shop and three restaurants are within walking distance, and the climate is benign all year. *Babies & over 12s welcome.*

Price	£250–£500 per week.
Rooms	6 cottages for 2.
Meals	Restaurants within walking distance.
Closed	Never.
Directions	Directions on booking.

Pippa Setton
North of Vilamoura,
8100-292 Loulé

Tel	+44 (0)1892 523031
Email	kazuriclub@tiscali.co.uk
Web	www.algarvegardencottage.co.uk

Entry 81   Map 5

Casa Caseta

Sultry resorts with white sand beaches, glittering marina, casino, nightlife, riding, tennis and the best golf courses in Portugal – all within a 20-minute drive. And if that sounds too sophisticated for you, there's the authentic old market town of Loulé just down the road. Here is your chance to stay in a classic, classy Algarvian villa up in the hills – a massive treat. Its owner is Desmond, once immersed in the worlds of property, boatbuilding, fashion and design, now a charming, humorous B&B host. Start the day in the wicker-chaired conservatory where a simple continental breakfast is served; move on to the beaches and Saturday's 'gypsy market' in Loulé; come home to manicured lawns and a beautiful pool. Shady trees, pretty planting, comfortable seating, a splashing fountain, fields all around and masses of sky – the setting is immaculate. As for bedrooms, they're traditional, stylish, luxurious – one upstairs with a sunny private terrace, another one opening to the garden. Elegant bathrooms are heaped with white towels. Book up for dinner in Loulé – Desmond knows all the fun places. Great value. *Min. two nights.*

Price	€75–€95.
Rooms	3: 2 doubles, 1 twin.
Meals	Restaurants 3km.
Closed	Rarely.
Directions	From Loulé, dir. Boliqueme, immed. right to Vale Telheiro. Continue straight, up to top; when tarmac ends, fork right onto gravel road. At 1st house, fork left, next house on left.

Desmond O'Power
Vale Telheiro,
8100-334 Loulé

Tel	+351 289 417661
Mobile	+351 964 348840
Email	desopower@gmail.com
Web	www.algarveruralbedandbreakfast.com

Quintassential Holiday Cottages

The road is steep but the views spilling over the Atlantic take your breath away – blue, sparkling, unbroken. This old Portuguese farmhouse and its outbuildings have been sensitively converted and extended. Rooms have a rustic, modern simplicity: solid wood furniture, pretty tiles, embroidered cushions, colourful pottery. There are wood-burning stoves and microwaves, shelves of books, private terraces and barbecues; it's sophisticated yet cosy. For complete privacy, choose Casa do Forno, the converted bread oven; tiny, gorgeous, intimate, it is the ultimate in ergonomic design. Although temptingly near lively beaches and Loulé town, it's hard to drag yourself away from those views: the roof terrace has a horizon-wide panorama from the foothills of Monchique all the way to the Algarve coast. A terraced garden, swimming pool, hot tub and shady patio bar add to the choice of places to linger; feel yourself unwind. Rosa and Mike welcome young families and have their own: there's a play park and tons of baby equipment, and nappies in the welcome pack! *Birdwatching holidays spring & autumn. Min. stay three nights.*

Price	£330-£825 per week.
Rooms	4 cottages for 2-4 (max. 13 people).
Meals	Restaurants 2-minute walk.
Closed	Rarely.
Directions	From Faro to Loulé. From Loulé north dir. Salir for two minutes. Detailed directions on booking.

Rosa Gulliver
Apartado 1161,
8101-904 Loulé

Tel	+351 289 463867
Mobile	+351 917 108187
Email	info@quintassential.com
Web	www.quintassential.com

Casa Borboleta

At last, somewhere so family-friendly you can bring the little ones and enjoy yourself too. A traditional quinta has been transformed into two self-catering cottages, each housing four comfortably and in some style – perfect for two families together. There's a great garden with plenty of sitting spaces, a play area for children and a fenced-in pool that bobs with inflatables. If they wish to spread their wings, Trafal beach – not far – is wide, golden, perfect for building sandcastles. Back home, enjoy lunch cooked over the traditional Portuguese barbecue, on a vine-shaded patio that catches the breeze. Extras include shared washing facilities in the old donkey house, water heated by solar power (which you are encouraged to reuse for dousing the plants) and piles of DVDs. Sitting rooms are big informal affairs with throws on sofas adding colour to simple walls and tiled floors; warmly decorated bedrooms have a rustic charm; good-sized kitchens are equipped to feed the hungry (and babies). Note: the restaurants of pretty Querença village will give house-chefs a break should they tire of cooking.

Price	From £380 per week.
Rooms	2 cottages for 4–6.
Meals	Restaurant 2km.
Closed	Rarely.
Directions	From Faro to Loulé. After 3rd r'bout (dual c'way becomes single), 1st right opp. garage. Up left to bandstand; straight; over 3 r'bouts onto Querença Rd; cont. to Clareanes; 1st right to Carvalho; 1.5km; on right.

Nick & Nikki Bartlett
5 Clemente, Carvalho,
8100-235 Loulé

Tel	+44 (0)1252 703613
Email	info@casaborboleta.com
Web	www.casaborboleta.com

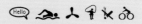

Casa Idalina

Not only is the house light, bright, well-designed and south-facing, it has a huge view over village and valley, and is a short hop from the coast and prized beaches. Set on a steep hillside, separated from others by carob and olive trees, the house is graced with numerous steps and terraces, each dotted with bougainvillea, lemon, yucca, small palms and bright annuals. In summer you'll be spending your days outside, on the cobbled barbecue terrace under the old olive tree or in the saltwater pool – fabulous. Inside is a large split-level, open-plan space divided into three: modern kitchen, dining room with big table and comfortable sitting room. Bedrooms are arranged in two wings, family-style: expect modern metal beds in most rooms, mirror-clad fitted wardrobes, white bathrooms with bright hand-painted tiles. Choose between the snazzy resorts to the west – Vilamoura, Vale do Lobo, Quinta do Lago – and the lesser known beaches to the east, and don't miss the flamingo island of Tavira. An illuminated pool, secure parking, satellite TV, WiFi and wood-burner complete the villa-perfect picture.

Price	£790–£1,520 per week.
Rooms	Villa for 8.
Meals	Restaurant 3km.
Closed	Never.
Directions	From São Brás de Alportel, main road for Loulé. After 4km, right for São Romão. Pass church on right; continue 400m, villa on right: name plaque on wall.

Alan & Carol Matthews
São Romão,
8150-058 São Brás de Alportel

Tel	+34 914 292115
Mobile	+34 637 450951
Email	alancarol@casa-idalina.com
Web	www.casa-idalina.com

Entry 85   Map 6

Monte do Casal

Here you have a low-lying Algarvian farmhouse in grand style, a stylish retreat for a gathering of the clans. The entrance sets the tone: impressive gates smothered in white azalea, a driveway edged by lush hedgerows, a carport under great palms. You will love the spacious interiors: the beamy old-fashioned country kitchen perfectly equipped, the sofa'd sitting room, the TV study, the antique-furnished corridor off which three bedrooms lie (two further rooms are by the pool). More treats outside: the gardens are lawned, secluded, surrounded by big trees, the swimming pool is gated and there's a lavishly furnished double veranda, a delicious spot for a lazy jug of Pimm's. Pretty mirrors, Sant' Anna tiles, cast-iron bedsteads, duck egg-blue shutters, statues of elephants on the terrace, a 17th-century well that supplies the house with fresh water... there's an atmosphere of faded splendour here, as much Anglo-French as Portuguese. The English manager runs the show, organises the gardener, the maids, the complementary first-night dinner, knows all the best restaurants, markets, beaches: his inside knowledge is invaluable.

Price	£1,600-£4,000 per week. Reduced prices for 2-6 in low season.
Rooms	Villa for 10.
Meals	Dinner on arrival. Restaurant 4km.
Closed	Never.
Directions	From Loulé, N270 dir. São Brás de Alportel. Opp. Zé Días restaurant follow sign to São Romão. Turn left just after church, house at bottom of hill.

Tamar Ferguson
São Romão,
8150-058 São Brás de Alportel

Tel	+44 (0)1228 543430
Email	montedocasal@hotmail.com
Web	www.montedocasal.net

Quinta Monte Serra

When Jean-Jacques bought this lovely old place, in among the carobs and the olives, his architect said, "change nothing." You'll forgive the new floors and windows – perfect replicas of the originals – and the old walls rendered with a deliberate rusticity. The 100-year-old farmhouse – built by an émigré who made his fortune in Brazil – lies a cobblestone's throw away from its outbuildings, one a fine white stable that once housed sheep and mules. Your host's relaxed personality is reflected in the informality and he's generous too: bikes on the house and bubbly in the fridge. Interiors are charming and uncluttered: solid country pieces, brown leather sofas, pretty vintage cast-iron beds; even the kitchens are inviting – we loved the Sant' Anna tiles. There are outdoor sitting areas for summer, wood-burners for winter and palm trees and peace all year round. As for the pool, it's a half moon-shaped beauty set into the old threshing floor. Have a splash, gaze on the sea… the beaches are a ten-minute drive (or mini-train ride). Brilliant for families, couples (the cottage is a sweet retreat) or a great big party of friends.

Price	Casarão €875–€1,645. Patio House €560–€980. Curral Branco €490–€1,050. Cottage €350–€560. Prices per week.
Rooms	Casarão for 6. Patio House for 4. Curral Branco for 4. Cottage for 2.
Meals	Restaurant 4km.
Closed	Rarely.
Directions	A22 exit 15 dir. Sta Catarina; right at Foupana sign. Straight to last Estirmantens sign, 8-sided sign left, on dirt track, to palm trees.

Jean-Jacques de Coninck
Estiramantens,
8800-504 Tavira

Tel	+351 281 961099
Mobile	+351 961 142562
Email	welcome@monte-serra.com
Web	www.monte-serra.com

Vilacampina Guesthouse

Watch the hoopoes feeding on the lawn as you tuck into tortillas, cheeses, croissants, cakes, tomatoes, figs and jams... breakfast is so scrumptious one guest was inspired to draw it. Behind the security gates and the minimalist glass walls you are pampered in five-star style, yet the place is so intimate and the staff so lovely, it retains the friendly feel of a guesthouse. This dazzling white villa stands in sharp contrast to the ancient olive trees and orange orchards beyond; all is utterly peaceful. The crisp feel continues indoors, the black, red and grey décor serene with a Japanese feel; the bedrooms are generous in comfort and size. From the art on the walls to the lavender bags for your clothes every detail is aimed to delight; there are books, DVDs and private terraces too. Pluck plums and apricots from the trees as you amble down to the cool blue pool, for white loungers and a shaded honesty bar stocked with beers and interesting liqueurs. Delightful staff are full of local knowledge: of Tavira, beautiful yet unspoilt, the fish restaurants of Olhão, the gorgeous beaches.

Price	€99–€170. Suite €140–€215.
Rooms	9: 2 doubles, 6 twins/doubles, 1 suite for 2.
Meals	Restaurant 5-minute drive.
Closed	January.
Directions	A22 exit 16 for Tavira. Right at 2nd r'bout dir. Olhão. 7km to Luz. 2nd road onto square; round to right & immed. left for Vilacampina. 2km then right; 1km, on right.

Sofia Moura Borges
Sítio da Campina, Luz de Tavira,
8880-107 Tavira

Tel   +351 281 961242
Email   vilacampina@mail.telepac.pt
Web   www.vilacampina.pt

Entry 88   Map 6

Quintamar

Here are four pretty apartments and houses perfect for family and friends; from the top floors you can see the sea. The interiors are tiled and spacious, with enough stripes and blocks of colour to add life to a functional décor. Quintamar sits in the Ria Formosa: lovely farmland and trees and a 15-minute walk to a boat (summer only) or train to ferry you to the sand-spit beaches – reputedly the finest in Portugal. But the main joy is the natural swimming pool whose plants keep the water pure; bathing is in the centre, away from dense waterlilies and singing frogs! Grown-ups can loll on loungers as little ones duck and dive, or join the owners' children on the wooden pirate ship. On arrival, kind Tamar brings you milk, fruit, rolls, jam and eggs from her hens, local chef Pedro cooks on request, and there are heaps of seafood restaurants in the fishing village of Sta Luzia. Beds – super comfy – are draped with Indian spreads, sofas wear throws, wood-burners keep you warm on cool nights, the two-storey apartments have sliding doors to balconies, and patios have space for barbecues. It couldn't be nicer.

Price	Houses €400-€950. Apartments €300-€850. Prices per week.
Rooms	2 houses for 6-8. 2 apartments for 5. Apartments can interconnect.
Meals	Chef available. Restaurant 1km.
Closed	Never.
Directions	From Tavira continue on N125 dir. Santa Luzia. At Pedras D'el Rei, turn left at Quintamar sign, follow signs on dirt track.

Tamar Welti
St Pedro 254-a,
8800-255 Tavira
Mobile   +351 963 345637
Email   quinta_mar@hotmail.com
Web   www.quintamar.com

Entry 89   Map 6

Casa Vale del Rei

Robin and Geraldine fell in love with a holiday guest house and came back to buy it. This handsome whitewashed farmhouse east of Tavira is surrounded by orange and olive groves and sweeping countryside views. Cabanas beach is a five-minute drive, three golf courses lie not much further. Not that you'll be in a hurry to explore; Casa Vale del Rei is heaven in summer with its waterlily ponds, fountains and shady corners, its lush groupings of oleander, lavender, palms, pines and lazy pool. Your friendly, helpful hosts have also created a stylish, contemporary interior without losing any authenticity. Bathrooms glisten white, bedrooms are cool and lofty with natural materials: muslin curtains, white-painted furniture, pretty cotton. Go for the romantic cabin for two with a white-stained wood interior and a private roof terrace. Sitting rooms are similarly spare, in cool creams and taupes, with stylish splashes from chandeliers, antiqued mirrors and fabric pictures. Help yourself to afternoon tea – and possibly cake – and take it to the shaded terrace; Robin does a proper cooked breakfast too.

Price	€90-€140.
Rooms	7: 2 doubles, 3 twins, 2 family rooms.
Meals	Restaurant 150m.
Closed	Rarely.
Directions	From Faro A22 for Espanha, exit 16 Tavira. At 2nd r'bout, N125 for Vila Real. Pass Eurotel on left, left at sign to Almargem. Left up track opposite white bridge on right.

Robin Ford-Jones
Almargem,
8800-053 Tavira

Tel	+351 281 323099
Email	casavaledelrei@hotmail.com
Web	www.casavaledelrei.co.uk

Monte do Álamo

Tavira has an array of wonderful restaurants – but why go out when you can eat in? Lovely Rosario brings the robust flavours of the Algarve and Alentejo to her quietly luxurious B&B, hosted outdoors by the barbecue or at the big mahogany table. She and her Columbian husband, both from large families, love welcoming guests into their home. Rosário knows too about the history and the landscape of the area and provides a booklet of walks – you're in perfect hands! As for the old farmhouse, it's been treated to an exemplary conversion: white walls and cool floors... all feels smart, sleek and serene. Bedrooms, away from the owners' quarters, are elegantly simple, with stylish square basins and big roomy showers; colours are subtle, fabrics textured and the huge suite gets its own terrace. In winter, settle into a squishy white sofa or a rattan armchair. In summer, find a roof terrace, a hammock, a bench under the carob tree: there are lots of places to sit in the shade, and you're high above the town so you catch the breezes. Views reach across Tavira to the sea. *Ask about courses in cookery & ceramics.*

Price	€80–€120. Suite €125–€145.
Rooms	5: 2 doubles, 2 twins/doubles, 1 suite.
Meals	Dinner €27.50.
Closed	Rarely.
Directions	A22 exit 16, over r'about dir. Tavira. After 3.5km, exit r'bout dir. Sta Margarida. Right for Fojo after 100m, after 800m right for Monte do Álamo. House on right.

Maria do Rosário Mesquita
Poço do Álamo,
8800-254 Tavira
Tel   +351 281 098209
Email   info@montedoalamo.net
Web   www.montedoalamo.net

Casa Beleza do Sul

Elegant but unintimidating, this airy multi-terraced *casa* is a privileged place to stay. In the maze-like centre of fascinating Tavira – near the old fish market, a stroll from the ferry – is this fine 19th-century townhouse exquisitely restored by its architect owner. Italian Paola has kept the handsome carved ceilings and the wood and mosaic floors; intact too is the paintwork on the doors, their refined colours matched with cool walls of burnished lime render; the effect is stunning. What's on offer are two apartments with kitchenettes (one with the bed on the mezzanine, the other with a spectacular ceiling) and a two-bedroom suite off a big, airy communal living room with a kitchen and a patio terrace. Don't expect total quiet; do expect a relaxing atmosphere amongst authentic Portuguese life: cafés, bars, shops and restaurants serving grilled fish so fresh it tastes of the sea. Or rustle up something simple at the Casa and take it to the lovely long roof terrace with views of terracotta rooftops and palm-fringed river front; if you're feeling nomadic, you can bed down and sleep under the stars. A rare gem.

Price	€50–€80. Apartment €60–€90 per night.
Rooms	1 + 2: 1 suite for 2-4. 2 apartments for 2-4.
Meals	Breakfast €5. Guest kitchen. Restaurants 100m.
Closed	Never.
Directions	From A22 exit 17 for Tavira, follow signs to Centro & continue to square with cinema. Small alley (Rua Dr. Parreira) to right of Pasteleria Tavirense, nº 43.

	Paola Boragine
	Rua Dr. Parreira 43,
	8800-346 Tavira
Tel	+351 960 060906
Email	mail@casabelezadosul.com
Web	www.casabelezadosul.com

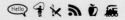

Quinta da Colina

An old Algarvian manor house – a rare treat. Architect George and wife Tassie, hospitable
and delightful, have done it up stylishly and love meeting guests. Here you can B&B or
self-cater; there are two bedrooms in the house – lofty beamed ceilings, white voile
curtains, a sparkling chandelier – two more in a separate house, and a studio apartment
that sleeps three. Not a frill or a flounce in sight, just cool white walls, shining floor tiles,
red leather sofas, attractive rugs... and several snazzy touches, in bathrooms and kitchens
and steel mezzanine stairs. The overwhelming feeling is one of space and perfect
proportions, while views stretch across the landscape – even from the shaded terraces
with which each building is blessed. This grand old house sits in a six-hectare estate of
olive, orange and carob trees, with paddocks for horses and, down the valley, a delicious
pool created from a former irrigation tank: square-shaped and rustically modern. Walks
and bike rides abound, you're car-minutes away from golf courses and beaches, and
atmospheric Tavira is a very short drive.

Price	€95–€135. Studio €125–€175 per night. House €525–€1,250 per week.
Rooms	1 + 2: 1 twin. Studio for 3. House for 4.
Meals	Restaurant 2km.
Closed	Rarely.
Directions	From Tavira N125 dir. Spain. Left for Almargem, right, over bridge. Continue through Almargem, left at junction signed Solteiras. Quinta 300m on left.

George Ritchie
Solteiras, Conceição,
8800-059 Tavira

Tel	+351 281 370604
Mobile	+351 913 813782
Email	quintadacolina@gmail.com
Web	www.quintadacolina.com

Companhia das Culturas

An Amazonian anthropologist, Eglantina brushes aside convention with ease. She has turned this 18th-century farm into something of an artist's residence: follow whitewashed corridors open to the sky and stars, as they thread their way to rustic rooms replete with mosaic tiling, exposed beams, glass globe lamps and ample beds. Some have slumbering mezzanines tucked into the eaves. Skylights filter through electric shutters, and behind opaque screens it's a mere step into bathrooms with chic cork-edged basins. There's a ragged kind of joy here: rusted girders splay artistically like trees in the courtyard and offer cooling shade; iron bedsteads arrange themselves around the pool; and, in the communal area, a huge olive press rises resplendent on a great plinth above the library and honesty bar. Fig, olive and almond trees unravel toward sleepy San Bartolomeu and offer a seasonal indication of your tantalising breakfast plate each morning: from dried tuna and wild rucola to smoked codfish liver, fresh goat's cheese and honey cakes. Young Luis may even present you with a clutch of carob leaves as you cycle down to the sea.

Price	€70–€130. Whole house: €2,500–€4,000 per week.
Rooms	7: 5 doubles, 2 suites for 2-3.
Meals	Dinner €15. Wine €15. Restaurants in Villa Real, 1km.
Closed	January.
Directions	A2 dir. Vila Real, exit for Monte Gordo. Left after 125m. Turn for Castro-Marim. After 700m follow sign for São Bartolemeu. Left at white church, 200m on right.

Eglantina Monteiro
Fazenda S. Bartolomeu,
8950-270 Castro Marim
Mobile   +351 969 379342
Email   companhiadasculturas@gmail.com
Web   www.companhiadasculturas.com

Casa Rosada

Staying here is like staying with friends… who just happen to run one of Europe's most exquisite B&Bs. This traditional mansion, flecked with dazzling modernity, sitting beneath the walls of a 13th-century fort, is a place to feel stylishly at home. Andrew used to be picture editor for Marie-Claire, hence the chandelier that drips glass grapes above bohemian armchairs, or the hall table seemingly plucked from a Restoration play. Meanwhile, in a bucolic kitchen, Rupert rustles up geranium-infused panna cotta and olive-oil cake that taste like sunshine on the tongue, and are best enjoyed in the fabulous garden amid the luxuriant fronds and honeysuckle archways. The upstairs bedrooms are sea-light and breezy, one boasting a four-poster tapering to bud-like points, the other spreading around a pampering bed, whose elegant bedspread slips silkily over warm limbs. The cool downstairs double is served by its own outside entrance and all have warmly tiled bathrooms with thoughtful glass trolleys for busy wash bags. Throw open shutters and let in sun and birdsong, idle chatter and the clatter of lunchtime dominoes.

Price	€80-€95.
Rooms	3 doubles.
Meals	Dinner, 3 courses, €25. Wine €8-€25. Restaurants 4km.
Closed	Rarely.
Directions	From Faro A22 for Espanha, exit 18 for Vila Real de S. Antonio. At 1st r'bout right into Castro Marim; 2nd left; thro' town. Pass Balneiros Publicos on right, right & immed. left; 2nd house on right.

Andrew Roberts
Rua Dr. Silvestre Falcao 6, 8, 10,
8950-128 Castro Marim
Tel   +351 281 544215
Email   casarosada1@mac.com
Web   www.casarosada-algarve.com

Madeira

Casas Valleparaízo

Nine snug lodges on an old fruit farm, set in magical gardens in the hills. Chestnuts, urze, gingko, pear trees, apple trees and bountiful fuchsias: the lushness of the vegetation reflects the hill climate. These pristine cottages are well-scattered, two of them new, the rest old farm buildings restored some years ago; all gleam. The décor is unfussy country style, the bathrooms are white, and each one has its own piece of garden for eating and lounging. We like two-storey Pindas with its carpeted bedroom under the eaves, and Levadinha for its open-plan layout. Leonor is the smiling housekeeper who greets you with Madeira and cake, Sofia runs the place with enjoyment and ease; her parents, once at the forefront of rural tourism, are still involved in revitalising local crafts. There's badminton and table tennis here and levada-walking beyond; the pebbles and pier of Canico are a ten-minute drive and it's a stroll to the nearest small restaurant; a great position. Cockerels and peacocks strut, blackcaps and firecrests trill and all feels tranquil, verdant and fresh. *Min. three nights. A Madeira Rural property.*

Price	€85–€130 per night.
Rooms	9 cottages: 6 for 2, 1 for 4, 2 for 6.
Meals	Breakfast €6, by arrangement. Restaurant 200m.
Closed	Never.
Directions	From airport R101 dir. Funchal, exit 15, right for Cancela; r'bout dir. Camacha, thro' tunnels. R'bout, left for Funchal; left past shopping centre. Right after yellow/grey bus stop.

Sofia Câmara
Vale Paraíso,
9135-060 Camacha

Tel	+351 962 939357
Email	info@valleparaizo.com
Web	www.valleparaizo.com

Quintinha de São João

It may be new but it looks historic; when you step inside you are transported to the England of *Brief Encounter*. The staff are delightful, everything feels tranquil, and there's an old-world formality about the main rooms: brass lamps with pleated shades on occasional tables, gleaming antique desks and gilt-framed oils, velvet armchairs, a grand piano. Each of the understatedly luxurious bedrooms has its own sitting area and charming local touches, such as carved wooden bedheads and island embroidery. Buffet breakfast, hot or cold, is displayed on snowy linen; dinners – al fresco once a week in summer – focus on Goan-Portuguese dishes accompanied by fine wines and taste divine. On the second floor a heated indoor pool looks to mountains and Funchal below. (You can walk steeply down into town, and catch the courtesy bus back.) Outside are ancient trees and lawns punctuated with palms, ferns and wrought-iron benches; flowers spill from urns, hydrangeas bloom in the shelter of low stone walls… best of all, there's a delicious spa with an outdoor pool and a stylish bar.

Price	€132–€182. Singles €95–€136. Suites €158–€234.
Rooms	43: 34 twins, 9 suites.
Meals	Dinner €32. Wine from €12–€35.
Closed	Never.
Directions	From airport, R101 for Funchal; exit 9, 3rd exit at r'bout; thro' tunnel. U-turn at r'bout & back thro' tunnel; right after Hotel Four Views Baía, 25m on right.

André Barreto
Rua da Levada de São João 4,
9000-191 Funchal

Tel	+351 291 740920
Email	info@quintinhasaojoao.com
Web	www.quintinhasaojoao.com

Casa do Papagaio Verde

Fresh flowers on the table, a glass of Madeira from housekeeper Vera, beaming warmth and generosity from start to finish. Filomena's architect-designed home is friendly open-plan and dotted with interesting arty pieces. Ground-floor rooms are large with wooden floors, big beds and fabrics sourced on the owner's Lisbon ventures, while a chrome staircase leads to a romantic suite, a honeymooners' paradise. Our favourite studios, Piscina and Oliveira, have their own turfed outdoor patch and stunning views of the garden sweeping down to the sea. Gaze oceanward as you breakfast on fresh rolls, exotic homemade jams (physalis, pitanga), fruit salads and pancakes. Speciality Madeiran dishes – picadinho stew, Alentejo chicken – topped off by fabulous desserts, fill the dinner menu. Chill under poolside palm trees or lose yourself in novels on super comfy armchairs. Playful dogs, the odd cat or goat roam too. Funchal city is close – explore its kaleidoscope-colourful morning markets, or dine out at the fantastic fish restaurant with a rooftop bar a short walk away. It's lovely. *A Madeira Rural property.*

Price	€60-€93. Apartments €60-€93 per night.
Rooms	3 + 4: 2 doubles, 1 suite. 4 apartments for 2.
Meals	Breakfast for self-caterers €7. Dinner €15. Wine €12.50. Restaurant 3km.
Closed	Never.
Directions	From airport, R101 for Funchal; exit 7 Santa Rita. Over r'bout, right after Hipomóveis; at recycling point, left, uphill; at fork, right, downhill. On left, 2nd grey gate.

	Filomena Babo
	São Martinho, Travessa do Papagaio Verde 31, 9000-656 Funchal
Tel	+351 291 775900
Email	casadopapagaio@netmadeira.com
Web	www.casadopapagaio.com

Entry 98   Map 5

Vila Marta

What you find here is all too rare: an apartment hotel with a family-run feel. Multi-lingual Joel is friendly and energetic with a delightful sense of humour, Dona Maria Jose is the smiling housekeeper, and the service is second to none. This new tiered complex is on the rapidly expanding edge of town, walking distance from bar, hypermarket and takeaway – perfect! Funchal is reachable by bus, car, taxi or brisk *levada* walk, the beach is a mile down the hill, and if you don't fancy the puff back up, Joel may collect you. The suites are traditional, comfortable, spotless and bright, each with a head-height wall dividing bedroom from living area, and a balcony with a view of the sea. There are white net curtains, framed watercolours, a hob, fridge-minibar, toaster and coffee maker, fresh rolls left each morning outside your door, a sofa, superb mattresses and cable TV: great attention to detail, and a late-checkout shower room. The plant-filled, gleamingly tiled 'winter garden', furnished with wicker chairs and glass-top tables, makes a very pleasant meeting place. *Min. two nights. A Madeira Rural property.*

Price	Studio €49-€71. Apartment €69-€89. Prices per night.
Rooms	9: 8 studios for 2, 1 apartment for 2.
Meals	Restaurants 2km.
Closed	Rarely.
Directions	From airport, R101 for Funchal; exit 8 for São Martinho. Left at fork, over viaduct to r'bout; 2nd exit, thro' tunnel; right at r'bout. Straight at next r'bout to sea, 1st right, on right.

Joel Alves
Travessa do Amparo 36,
9000-647 Funchal

Tel	+351 291 768200
Mobile	+351 968 073419
Email	vilamarta@netmadeira.com
Web	www.vila-marta.com

Quinta da Bela Vista

A manor house with exquisite formal walled gardens and sweeping views of Funchal Bay: relax with a drink or a snack from the bar and unwind. Huge centenarian trees line the cobbled paths that link these three buildings: quinta, restaurant and annexe. Expect fabulous antiques and few flaws in this multi-starred hotel where the Swedish royals stay. Bedrooms in the main house are classic in feel with warm colours; rooms in the annexe are less atmospheric, with a modern feel. Attentive staff can serve breakfast on your private terrace; just ask. The conservatory-style restaurant, bright with yellow walls, delivers refined dishes to elegant tables; à la carte is an option in the dining room of the manor. There's a billiard room, a card room, a library, a small fitness room with a jacuzzi and sauna, and hushed lounges with open fires in winter. Outside are a tennis court and a pool, elegantly floodlit at night. Should you like to go snorkelling or scuba diving, trips can be arranged; and there's a courtesy bus to Funchal. Or make the most of the hotel's yacht and drop in on the local islands. Bliss.

Price	€220–€512.
Rooms	89: 82 twins/doubles, 7 suites.
Meals	Dinner, 3 courses, €42.50.
Closed	Never.
Directions	From airport, R101 for Funchal; exit 9 for Cam. do Pilar, 1st left; 1st right for Funchal centre. Continue to pink wall; road signed Pavilhão do Cab, to Caminho do Avista Navios, 2nd gate on yellow wall.

Gonçalo Monteiro
Caminho do Avista Navios 4,
9000-129 Funchal

Tel	+351 291 706400
Email	info@belavistamadeira.com
Web	www.belavistamadeira.com

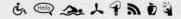

Estalagem da Ponta do Sol

With a history still sticky from the island's sugar trade — Madeira was once the world's first exporter of 'white gold' — this self-styled 'escape hotel', a bold departure from the rustic island cliché, retains little vestige of the quinta that used to be here (you arrive via a red-lit elevator from the village below, for starters). Award-winning, über minimalist architectural lines lead you to open-plan, split-level interiors; wooden flooring, lots of glass, dashing art on the walls. A large grassy terrace, originally for whale-spotting, dominated by an ancient dragon tree, overlooks the village below. Above, accessed by a funky footbridge, is the bedroom block; blacks, whites and greys, huge beds, huge mirrors, designer chairs, black-and-white rural landscapes, cathedral windows to balconies and views to die for. (It's like sleeping in a design magazine on a cliff!) Take a bath in the spa or loll in the infinity pool, the bay spread prettily at your feet, the wind in the palms, a glass of fine local wine in your hand and the kids at home... try and come up with reasons to leave. It's cool, and it knows it.

Price	€90–€130.
Rooms	54 twins/doubles.
Meals	Half-board €22 pp extra. Packed lunch €8.
Closed	Never.
Directions	From Funchal R101, exit 1 for Ribeira Brava. 3 tunnels, before 4th, left at r'bout. Estalagem on top of cliff; look for elevator tower.

André Diogo
Quinta da Rochinha, Ponta do Sol,
9360-529 Funchal

Tel	+351 291 970200
Email	info@pontadosol.com
Web	www.pontadosol.com

Vila Afonso

From high on the island's southern coast, the garden looks over an entrancing jumble of banana groves, vineyards and rooftops to the intense blue of the Atlantic far below. It's a view you won't forget. The family has been here for generations but the mellow old stone building goes back to the 17th century. This is where guests stay (the Afonsos occupy a newer house next door, on the other side of a little pool with a retractable roof). The B&B rooms are traditional: shining wood, pastel walls, lush house plants and a few antiques. Beds range from wrought-iron to an elegant four-poster; bathrooms are spotless. This family farm and vineyard cover just over one acre, and the garden is equally irreproachable. Statues are dotted around vivid lawns criss-crossed with paths and an explosion of exotica: passionfruit, strelitzia, white plume grasses, tall bay trees and the floss silk tree on which the Monarch butterfly feeds. In the atmospheric cobbled adega, Madeira wine tastings take place once a week – your chance to buy a 1957 vintage! A very welcoming place where you can do your own thing. *A Madeira Rural property.*

Price	€60–€79.
Rooms	4 + 2: 2 doubles, 2 twins. 2 bungalows for 2-4.
Meals	Restaurant 5-minute walk.
Closed	Rarely.
Directions	From airport R101, 2nd sign to Câmara de Lobos, 5th exit. Right onto main street João Gonçalves Zarco. Follow signs for Estreito de Câmara de Lobos. Keep on road.

João Afonso
Estrada João Gonçalves Zarco 574-B,
9325-033 Estreito de Câmara de Lobos

Tel	+351 291 911510
Mobile	+351 919 269778
Email	info@vilaafonso.com
Web	www.vilaafonso.com

Fajã dos Padres

Twelve out of ten for approach! You reach the houses down a 250m vertical cliff face, in a panoramic, glass-fronted lift. "An island within the island", they call it, this fertile volcanic terrace between cliff and sea, cultivated since the discovery of Madeira. An organic Garden of Eden-esque plantation envelops you, rich with mango, banana, papaya and avocados the size of pumpkins. The houses are architect restored and delightfully different, from 'Marinheiro', characterful with antiques and beautiful granite kitchen, to open-plan 'Casa das Vinhas' themed in whites and blues; all have patios and wooden loungers facing the sea. Bream and wrasse frolic in the super-clear waters off the bathing jetty and beach; Malvasia grapes line the path to the palm-fringed restaurant/bar – you might spot a VIP sipping mango juice at sunset. Lunch is served with a smile, but no evening meals so enjoy the peace, broken by the waves rolling onto the rocky foreshore and the calls of the shearwaters. For sightseeing and supplies, it's a short hop by sea taxi to Funchal and Ribeira Brava. Bliss for adventurers. *A Madeira Rural property.*

Price	€80-€100 per night.
Rooms	7 houses for 2, 1 studio for 2.
Meals	Breakfast €6-€9. Lunch €15. Wine €18. Meals can be delivered to door.
Closed	Mid-January to end-February.
Directions	From airport, R101 for Funchal; exit 3 to Quinta Grande; left at x-roads (brown sign), follow bend in road to right, car park at cliff edge.

Patricia & Pedro Jardim Fernandes
Estrada Padre António Dinis Henriques 1,
9300-261 Quinta Grande

Tel	+351 291 944538
Email	info@fajadospadres.com
Web	www.fajadospadres.com

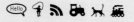

Casa do Retiro

The honesty bar holds bottles of vintage Madeira: it's that sort of place. This new-but-traditional house was built on the family plot some years ago, and the feeling is one of understated privilege and cosy luxury. English, Indo-Portuguese and Madeiran antiques prevail: great grandfather's bed is dressed with monogrammed sheets, there are chestnut chairs, a lovely ceramic lamp over the dining table and wine glasses in a mahogany cabinet. Dona Graça, the delightful maid, looks after it all. Such is the grandeur you'd imagine families would not be welcome but no, there's a games room, an inflatable child's pool next to the big one, and the big one is fenced. Indeed, the whole garden is child-safe, and filled with unusual trees loved by birds; through their branches you can glimpse Ponta do Sol. There's a kitchen with an island worktop and a barbecue with a tiled table, and if you tire of cooking, scoot across the road to the pizzeria. In Madalena do Mar (6km) are fish restaurants lining the promenade, and pebble beaches; and the bustling village of Canhas is up the road. *Min. four nights. A Madeira Rural property.*

Price	€95–€110 for 2. €14 for each additional adult. Under 6s free. Prices per night.
Rooms	House for 9 (+ 2 cots).
Meals	Pizzeria 50m.
Closed	Never.
Directions	From airport, R101 for Funchal; exit 1 Ribeira Brava; follow Ponta do Sol. Right at fountain r'bout; into Canhas; right immed. after Teresinhas Monument, on right.

Tito Noronha
Rua Serrado da Cruz,
9360-311 Canhas

Mobile	+351 963 337153
Email	casadoretiro@hotmail.com

Entry 104   Map 5

Madeira

B&B & Self-catering

Quinta das Vinhas

Stay at one of the oldest manor houses on the island. It is flanked by mountains, surrounded by vineyards and has views that sweep to the sea. This 17th-century homestead is deeply atmospheric with flagstone floors, wooden ceilings and hand-painted tiles. The dining room, where friendly, helpful staff ferry good food to convivial tables, is in the former kitchen, and the prayer room is a reading room; both are delightful with elegant antiques. The peaceful, gracious atmosphere extends to the lush grounds; stroll among the angel's trumpets, dream to the song of the canaries, play boules under the ancient oaks as your children clamber up the tulip tree, cool off in the pools. Then back for a glass of the Quinta's very fine madeira. Bedrooms in the main house have traditional furnishings and are flooded with light; the apartments, well set apart and newly built of Madeiran stone, have comfortable country interiors and bold colours. You can fish from the village pier, take a dip in the sea, walk the nearby Levada Nova, pluck a passionfruit from a tree. A happy place. *Min. two to seven nights. A Madeira Rural property.*

Price	€60–€90. Cottages from €390 per week.
Rooms	6 + 14: 6 doubles. 14 cottages for 2-3. Extra beds available.
Meals	Dinner €16.50. Pool snacks available in summer.
Closed	Never.
Directions	From Funchal R101 dir. Ponte do Sol; exit at 2 r'bouts for Calheta. Thro' 2 tunnels; at r'bout, exit for Prazeres. Right at 2nd sign for Est da Calheta, 800m.

Isabel Welsh Talas
Lombo dos Serrões - Estº Calheta,
9370-221 Calheta

Tel	+351 291 824086
Email	info@qdvmadeira.com
Web	www.qdvmadeira.com

Entry 105   Map 5

Madeira, Porto Santo, the Desertas and Selvagens Islands

Nature, breathtaking landscape and fascinating culture, all in a mild climate

In the middle of the Atlantic Ocean lie Europe's most exotic islands: the archipelago of Madeira, 450 miles south of Portugal and 600 miles from the Portuguese capital, Lisbon.

For visitors, the options are as varied as the scenery: monuments, historic squares and streets, enchanting gardens, pretty hamlets, stunning landscapes, impressive volcanic caves, dramatic coastlines and unspoilt beaches.

Climate

Madeira is envied for its sub-tropical climate: temperatures hover around 23°C in summer and 17°C in winter; water temperatures reach 23°C in summer and 18°C in winter.

History

The island of Porto Santo was the first area discovered, by João Gonçalves Zarco and Tristão Vaz Teixeira, in 1419. A year later, those two navigators arrived on Madeira, accompanied by Bartolomeu Perestrelo. Colonisation of the archipelago started around 1425.

Culture

Madeira is rich in culture and tradition and all year round you can enjoy a vast range of events, many of which are centred around the archipelago's gastronomic heritage.

Nature and landscape

The archipelago has a large number of nature reserves and natural parks that support a rich variety of flora and fauna. Walkers will delight in the trails along the levadas – waterways that go around and across the mountains – that were manmade at the time of colonisation.

Madeira Rural is a not-for-profit association that offers a choice of excellent quality accommodation in rural cottages and in islanders' homes. The association has an online booking option and lots of useful travel information.

www.madeirarural.com

Portugal is a foodie's delight. We take you on a gastronomic romp through the country's regions.

Minho

Minho is famous for the young drinking wine, vinho verde, for corn bread, 'broa de milho', and for 'caldo verde', a soup of cabbage, onion, potato and chouriço. The meat is offally good (old joke) especially the unusual piggy bits – try 'arroz de sarrabulho' made with rice and pig's blood – and fish on the coast, even eels if you're brave... Meat is cooked in wood-fired ovens; mountain goat is a speciality, and is not the only rare breed: the brown Arouquessa and curly-horned Cachena make good beef cattle.

'Doces conventuais' are confections/patisseries invented in the convents made from egg yolk (said to be left over after the nuns starched their habits with the whites), sugar and ground almonds. Minho is also home to 'arroz doce', rice pudding which comes with cinnamon, maybe lemon – a traditional family Christmas dish.

Trás-os-Montes

Home to the pig breed Bísaro (tasty) and Barrosa beef (equally tasty). Note that 'alheira', despite appearances, is not pork, but spiced game/chicken sausage made by Jews keeping kosher in secret under the Inquisition, hoping to be isolated and unmolested in this rustic corner of Portugal. 'Cozido à Portuguesa' is the ultimate in peasant food: a one-pot dish of sausage, chicken, ham, beef, vegetables, broth, potatoes... Corn, chestnuts and sausage stock the cupboards. The towns of Chaves and Murça hold fortnightly markets – heaven for foodies.

Douro

The Douro Gorge is the wine-river home to the vines from which port grapes tumble, known for wine, wine and more wine. To accompany it try roast meats such as 'cabrito' (kid), 'cordeiro' (lamb) and 'vitela' (veal). Local dishes include, from Lamego, smoked ham and sausage. Northern flavours feature soup and meat, lots of cumin and generous quantities of olive oil. For sweet things, Mesão Frio has chestnuts and Torre de Moncorvo sugared almonds. Cherries, citrus fruits, almonds and figs flourish.

Porto is undergoing a culinary renaissance. A host of fresh sea fish floods the market daily: sea bream ('pargo'), sole, swordfish, tuna, sea bass ('robalo'), monkfish, sardines etc, usually served grilled, or in a delectable fish stew, 'caldeirada de peixe' while prawns, lobster, squid, octopus and barnacles ('percebes') can feature in the 'cataplana,' named after the dish in which it is cooked. Fish is often prepared with pig lard, which competes with olive oil as Portugal's favourite fat. Tripe, and lots of it, is served with white beans. 'Francesinha' is a cheese-topped meat sandwich in a sauce of tomato, chilli and brandy.

Beiras

The dish of Portugal: 'leitão da Bairrada',

suckling pig, draws crowds to the town of Mealhada. 'Torresmos' are pork cracklings and 'morcela' is blood sausage, both by-products and both delicious. The Beiras have plenty of famous cheeses, like the runny, buttery 'queijo Serra da Estrela'. Pumpkin jam is delicious with the fresh white 'requeijão' produced during cheese-making, and the Beira Baixa boasts 'amarelo da Beira Baixa' made with ewe's milk, a semi-soft cheese.

Aviero is one of the few places where you can still see 'bacalhau de cura amarela', salt cod dried traditionally in the open air; wild duck comes from the marshes. Local sweet delicacies include 'ovos moles de Aveiro', egg yolks and sugar in little boats.

Alentejo

A vast region: animals in the north, arable farms in the south (vines, olives). Expect simple peasant food, and big portions! The rustic, bready stew, 'açorda', is a typically starchy dish made with vegetables, stale bread cubes, good stock and, these days, meat or fish. Wild boar ('javali') gorges on the same acorns as the fêted black pig, the 'porco preto', which grazes underneath the cork oak trees and produces exquisite 'presunto'. It's a piggy place: ears, tongues and trotters feature, and lots of bacon fat is used in cooking.

On the coast, the shark-like 'sopa de cação' – dogfish bread soup – is made with garlic, olive oil and herbs, and there are oysters, too. Inland, find bean stews, hare, game, and 'migas,' the dry, fatty, deep-fried

breadcrumb dish. The Arrábida hills yield honey. Cheeses include Évora, Mestiço de Toloso, Nisa, Serpa, all made with natural thistle rennet. But the real star is 'queijo de Azeitão' from the Setúbal Peninsula – soft, buttery and best served with 'marmelada', the famous quince jam.

Estremadura

The coast is fringed with fishing villages, so it's no surprise fisherman's soup is popular ('sopa de mariscos') and stew as well ('caldeirada de peixe'). 'Escabeche' is fish fried and dressed with vinaigrette and parsley, and 'batatas à murro' – bashed potatoes – are an inspired creation, roasted, squashed and garnished with fresh garlic. Heavenly melons come from Estremadura, as well as apples, peaches and 80% of Portugal's pears.

Lisbon

The ever-present salt cod appears in 'bacalhau à brás', tossed with deep-fried potato and scrambled egg. 'Bife com ovo à cavalo' is steak with an egg on top ("on horseback"), in sauce with chips. Many dishes are deep-fried, such as 'ovos verdes', an egg dish; salt cod slices – 'pataniscas de bacalhau'; and even the vegetables, such as 'peixinhos da horta' ("little fish from the garden"): green beans deep-fried in batter.

'Pastéis de nata', custard in sweet pastry cups, is a mouthwatering speciality whose fame has spread far beyond Portugal's borders.

Ribatejo

This region has some of the best olives and olive oil in Portugal. At the festival of Magusto in August the first casks are broached and the fermented grape juice tasted. Beans, pulses, soups and stews are delicious and popular; the more pig bits added the better. Fish: try river eels from the Tagus. The 'porco preto' black pigs live around here, too, and the local cuisine includes their ham. In Tomar, the sweet pastry 'fatia' is made – with just sugar and eggs.

Algarve

The 'cataplana' mentioned above (see Douro) originates here; understandable as the coast teems with seafood and shellfish: clams, oysters, octopus, stuffed squid, tasty baby cuttlefish ('choquinhos') and, of course, sardines. (Tuna is a familiar sight, but is now imported from Madeira.) The piri piri spice from Angola and Mozambique is used to prepare the grilled chicken dish 'frango à piri piri'. Lemons, tangerines, oranges, figs and almonds arrived with the Moors and never left, while sweet things include 'doces de amêndoa', almond paste sweets made into fruit, flowers, vegetables, every thinkable shape – another remnant of Moorish occupation. Fruit and veg include sweet potatoes, tomatoes, bananas, and the region has its own special goat's cheese: 'queijo da cabra do Algarve'.

Madeira

The impact of Madeira's status as a key stop-off on major trade routes is reflected in its cuisine. Expect tuna steaks on every menu, home-grown bananas, and the famous heated, fortified and aged Madeira wine. An 'espetada' is a kebab with pieces of meat or fish, sometimes served huge for a whole table to share, while the sea also yields limpets, cooked in garlic butter. Even here it's hard to escape pork, appearing in 'carne vinha d'alhos'. Exotic produce like 'anonas' (custard apples), guavas and mangos are everywhere, while sweet potato is used to make 'bolo de caco' bread. Spices from afar blend with molasses in the cake called 'bolo de mel'.

For many years Alastair Sawday Publishing has been 'greening' the business in different ways. Our aim is to reduce our environmental footprint as far as possible and with almost everything we do we have environmental implications in mind. In recognition of our efforts we won a Business Commitment to the Environment Award in 2005, a Queen's Award for Enterprise in the Sustainable Development category in 2006, and the Independent Publishers Guild Environmental Award in 2008.

The buildings

Beautiful as they were, our old offices leaked heat, used electricity to heat water and rooms, flooded spaces with light to illuminate one person, and were not ours to alter.

So in 2005 we created our own eco offices by converting some old barns to create a low-emissions building. Heating and

Photos: Tom Germain

lighting the building, which houses over 30 employees, now produces only 0.28 tonnes of carbon dioxide per year – a reduction of 35%. Not bad when you compare this with the six tonnes emitted by the average UK household. We achieved this through a variety of innovative and energy-saving building techniques, some of which are described below.

Insulation By laying insulating board 90mm thick immediately under the roof tiles and on the floor, and lining the inside of the building with plastic sheeting, we are now insulated even for Arctic weather, and almost totally air-tight.

Heating We installed a wood pellet boiler from Austria in order to be largely fossil-fuel free. The heat is conveyed by water to all corners of the building via an underfloor system.

Water We installed a 6,000-litre tank to collect rainwater from the roofs. This is pumped back, via an ultra-violet filter, to lavatories, shower and basins. There are also two solar thermal panels on the roof providing heat to the one hot-water cylinder.

Lighting We have a mix of low-energy lighting – task lighting and up lighting – and have installed three sun pipes.

Electricity Our electricity has long come from the Good Energy Company and is 100% renewable.

Materials Virtually all materials are non-toxic or natural, and our carpets are made from (80%) Herdwick sheep wool from National Trust farms in the Lake District.

Doors and windows Outside doors and new windows are wooden, double-glazed and beautifully constructed in Norway. Old windows have been double-glazed.

More greenery

Besides having a building we are proud of, and which is pretty impressive visually, too, we work in a number of other ways to reduce the company's overall environmental footprint.

- office travel is logged as part of a carbon sequestration programme, and money for compensatory tree planting donated to SCAD in India for a tree-planting and development project

- we avoid flying and take the train for business trips wherever possible
- car sharing and the use of a company pool car are part of company policy, with recycled cooking oil used in one car and LPG in the other
- organic and Fair Trade basic provisions are used in the staff kitchen and organic and/or local food is provided by the company at all in-house events
- green cleaning products are used throughout
- kitchen waste is composted on our allotment
- the allotment is part of a community garden – alongside which we keep a small family of pigs and hens

However, becoming 'green' is a journey and, although we began long before most companies, we realise we still have a long way to go.

Alastair Sawday has been publishing books for over twenty years, finding Special Places to Stay in Britain and abroad. All our properties are inspected by us and are chosen for their charm and individuality. Now, with twenty-four titles to choose from, there are plenty of places to explore. You can buy any of our books at a reader discount of 35%* on the RRP.

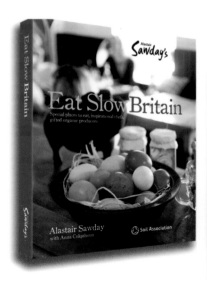 

www.sawdays.co.uk/bookshop

List of titles:	RRP	Discount price
British Bed & Breakfast	£14.99	£9.74
British Bed & Breakfast for Garden Lovers	£19.99	£12.99
British Hotels & Inns	£14.99	£9.74
Pubs & Inns of England & Wales	£15.99	£10.39
Venues in Britain	£11.99	£7.79
Cotswolds	£9.99	£6.49
Devon & Cornwall	£9.99	£6.49
Wales	£9.99	£6.49
Ireland	£12.99	£8.44
French Bed & Breakfast	£15.99	£10.39
French Self-Catering	£14.99	£9.74
French Châteaux & Hotels	£14.99	£9.74
French Vineyards	£19.99	£12.99
Paris	£9.99	£6.49
Green Europe	£11.99	£7.79
Italy	£14.99	£9.74
Portugal	£12.99	£7.79
Spain	£15.99	£9.74
Morocco	£9.99	£6.49
India	£11.99	£7.79
Go Slow England & Wales	£19.99	£12.99
Go Slow France	£19.99	£12.99
Go Slow Italy	£19.99	£12.99
Eat Slow Britain	£19.99	£12.99

*postage and packaging is added to each order

How to order:
You can order online at: www.sawdays.co.uk/bookshop/
or call: +44(0)1275 395431 and quote 'Reader Discount'

Quick reference indices

Wheelchair-accessible
These places tell us that they have at least one bedroom and bathroom that are accessible for wheelchair users. Please check details with owner before booking.

Minho 4
Douro 11
Beira 24 • 28
Estremadura 38 • 41 • 43 • 45
Alentejo 51 • 53 • 55 • 60
Algarve 62 • 67 • 68 • 69 • 75 • 82 • 87
Madeira 96 • 100 • 101 • 104

Singles
These places have a single room OR rooms are let to single guests for half the double room rate, or under.

Douro 20
Beira 26 • 27 • 33
Alentejo 54
Algarve 87

Budget
These places have rooms for £70 or under.

Minho 2 • 3 • 5
Douro 12 • 14
Beira 23 • 24 • 26 • 27 • 30 • 31 • 32 • 33 • 34
Estremadura 37 • 38 • 39 • 41
Alentejo 51 • 56 • 60 • 61
Algarve 68 • 69 • 70 • 71 • 75 • 77 • 78 • 82 • 87 • 92

Madeira 96 • 98 • 99 • 102 • 105

Pool
These places have a pool on the premises, use may be by arrangement.

Minho 1 • 3 • 5 • 6 • 7 • 8
Douro 11 • 12 • 13 • 14 • 15 • 16 • 17 • 18 • 19 • 20
Beira 21 • 22 • 25 • 26 • 27 • 28 • 29 • 30 • 31 • 32 • 33 • 36
Estremadura 37 • 38 • 39 • 41 • 42
Ribatejo 48
Alentejo 49 • 50 • 51 • 52 • 53 • 54 • 55 • 56 • 58 • 59 • 60
Algarve 62 • 63 • 64 • 65 • 67 • 68 • 69 • 70 • 71 • 72 • 73 • 74 • 75 • 76 • 77 • 78 • 79 • 80 • 81 • 82 • 83 • 84 • 85 • 86 • 87 • 88 • 89 • 90 • 93 • 94
Madeira 97 • 98 • 100 • 101 • 102 • 104 • 105

No car?
Property is within 10 miles of a bus/coach/train station and owner can arrange collection.

Minho 3 • 8
Douro 14 • 18
Beira 23 • 24 • 26 • 27 • 28 • 29 • 31 • 32
Estremadura 37 • 38 • 43 • 44 • 45
Ribatejo 48
Alentejo 49 • 51 • 53 • 54 • 55 • 57 • 58 • 60 • 61

Algarve 67 • 69 • 71 • 72 • 75 •
76 • 78 • 79 • 83 • 87 • 88 •
89 • 90 • 91 • 92 • 94
Madeira 99 • 101 • 103

Working farm
or vineyard

Minho 2 • 3 • 4 • 5 • 6 • 7 • 8
Douro 11 • 12 • 13 • 14 • 15 •
16 • 17
Beira 24 • 25 • 27 • 29 • 36
Estremadura 41
Alentejo 49 • 51 • 53 • 54 •
55 • 58 • 60
Algarve 62 • 63 • 66 • 76 • 80 •
91 • 94
Madeira 103 • 105

Photo: Monte do Álamo, entry 91

Wine
These properties are in
a wine-producing region.

Minho 2 • 3 • 5 • 6 • 8
Douro 11 • 12 • 14 • 17 • 18 •
19 • 20
Beira 23 • 24 • 25 • 26 • 30 •
31 • 32 • 33 • 34 • 35
Estremadura 37 • 38
Alentejo 49 • 50 • 51 • 52 •
53 • 55 • 56
Algarve 67 • 70 • 71 • 72 • 75 •
76 • 77 • 78 • 79 • 82 • 90
Madeira 102 • 103 • 105

Quick reference indices

Photo: Casa das Penhas Douradas Design Hotel, entry 28

Photo: Casa do Castelo Novo, entry 31

② Hotel   ① Estremadura

As Janelas Verdes

③ In the old city, just yards from the Museum of Ancient Art, is an aristocratic townhouse, 19th-century home of the novelist Eça de Queirós. It's the perfect place to lay your head when in Lisbon and from the moment you are greeted by smiling Palmira you feel like an honoured guest. To one side of the reception are a handsome fireplace, a piano and comfortable chairs, and marble-topped tables for breakfast in winter. Summer breakfasts – and candlelit aperitifs – are enjoyed on a cobbled patio where a fountain gurgles and bougainvillea runs riot. Inside, a grand old spiral staircase lined with Bordalo Pinheiro cartoons takes you up to bedrooms comfortable and quietly charming. Expect Portuguese repro beds, smart curtains, pale carpets, pastel colours, dressing gowns and towels embroidered with the JV logo. (And instead of a 'do not disturb' sign there's a hand-embroidered pillow that says 'shhh!'). Some rooms have impressive views of the river Tejo – book early if you want one. A delectable small hotel, enlarged to include a cosy library on the top floor with an honesty bar and a lovely convivial feel.

④	Price	€157–€298. Singles €143–€280.
⑤	Rooms	29 twins/doubles.
⑥	Meals	Breakfast €14. Restaurants nearby.
⑦	Closed	Never.
⑧	Directions	A2 over river Tejo, exit for Alcântara. Over r'bout; follow tram route for 500m. Hotel on right, close to Museu de Arte Antiga. Cais Rocha tramline five-minute walk.

The Cardoso & Fernandes Families
Rua das Janelas Verdes 47,
1200-690 Lisbon

Tel   +351 213 968143
Email   janelas.verdes@heritage.pt
Web   www.heritage.pt

⑨    ⑩ Entry 43   Map 3